TORTS
AND
SPORTS

Recent Titles from QUORUM BOOKS

TORTS AND SPORTS

Legal Liability in Professional and Amateur Athletics

RAYMOND L. YASSER

Quorum Books

Westport, Connecticut · London, England

Library of Congress Cataloging in Publication Data

Yasser, Raymond L.
   Torts and sports.

   Includes bibliographies and index.
   1. Liability for sports accidents—United States.
2. Sports—Law and legislation—United States.   I. Title.
KF1290.S66Y37   1985   346.7303'32   84-24948
ISBN 0-89930-092-8 (lib. bdg.)   347.306332

Library of Congress Catalog Card Number: 84-24948
ISBN: 0-89930-092-8

First published in 1985 by Quorum Books

Greenwood Press
A division of Congressional Information Service, Inc.
88 Post Road West, Westport, Connecticut 06881

Printed in the United States of America

10 9 8 7 6 5 4 3 2 1

The book is dedicated to my wife Lynn, and children Abram and Elizabeth. A secure loving environment is the best working environment. They provided me with that.

Contents

Preface

In writing this book I have managed to combine business with pleasure. By trade, I am a happily employed torts professor. For fun, I play sports, watch sports, and talk sports. Applying tort law principles to sports activities is therefore a rather natural preoccupation. Almost everywhere I am, torts are lurking about, begging to be litigated. So torts in sports is what I often see.

I feel confident that there are others out there who would be interested in sharing my admittedly peculiar reality. I anticipate an audience of lawyer-jocks, or jock-lawyers, as the case may be. For this audience, my book will be worthwhile. Tort law principles are reviewed in the most palatable of contexts. I have endeavored to keep these reviews crisp, accurate, and understandable—the short summary lecture your law professors rarely delivered. The application of the principles to sports cases is akin to a misdirection play. By the time you're finished reading the book, you will have thoroughly reviewed tort law without even knowing it. You will have also added to your own sports-torts collection. The news-grabbing cases like *Dale Hackbart v. "Boobie" Clark*, *Rudy Tomjanovich v. The Los Angeles Lakers*, and *Bill Walton v. Dr. Cook* are examined, along with the somewhat obscure but fascinating cases like *Virgil v. Time, Inc.* or *Spahn v. Julian Messner, Inc.*

The book is also designed for use in the classroom. Teachers in the area of sports and law will find the book to be a suitable text to cover material in the general area of civil liability. I also think that sports administrators will find the book to be a useful guide for avoiding tort liability.

I have struggled to make the book readable. I say "struggled" because readability appears to not have a high value in traditional legal writing. I have, for example, written a footnote-free manuscript. I have always believed that footnotes separate from the text are an evil to be avoided at all costs. I must admit I have never understood why lawyers are so committed to their use. Since this is my book, I have chosen not to use footnotes. Citations and references to other works are therefore included in the text. Afterthoughts which are often the grist of extended footnotes are either woven into the text, included in the additional notes section, or omitted entirely because of their inherent unworthiness in the final analysis. Moreover, attribution is provided for all quoted material, but repeated page references to the original source are avoided in the interest of readability.

To further facilitate readability, and to economize on the use of words, I take this opportunity to point out that forthwith only shorthand references will be made to the following oft-cited works. From now on, *The Law of Sports* by John C. Weistart and Cym Lowell (New York: Bobbs-Merrill, 1979) will be referred to as "Weistart and Lowell." Sports-minded lawyers should be familiar with this seminal work. The Restatement of Torts, Second, will be referred to as the "Restatement." The Uniform Commercial Code will be noted as the "UCC." The *Handbook of the Law of Torts* (4th ed.) by William Prosser (West Publishing, 1971) will be cited simply as "Prosser." It should also be noted that I took the liberty of republishing portions of my own work. Much of the introductory material on defamation in Chapter 5 is drawn from an article I wrote entitled, "Defamation as a Constitutional Tort: With Actual Malice for All," which appeared in 12 TULSA LAW JOURNAL 601 (1977). Some of the material concerning worker's compensation is drawn from an article I wrote entitled, "Are Scholarship Athletes at Big-Time Programs Really University Employees?-You Bet They Are!" which appeared in 9 BLACK LAW JOURNAL 65 (1984).

The format I follow divides each chapter into five distinct sections. Each chapter begins with introductory comments that broadly outline the relevant substantive law and set the stage for what follows. The second section, entitled "landmark cases," contains either edited extracts from leading cases or my own surveys of the case law. In the edited extracts, my comments appear in brackets. The third section is an in-depth look at an important case or an important topic in light of the preceding material. The fourth section, "additional notes," is aimed at raising pertinent issues related to the subject matter of the chapter. Finally, each chapter contains a bibliography of the best of the available legal literature.

Acknowledgments

This book would not have been possible without the help and encouragement of a great number of people. I would like to thank our university administration for permitting me to teach sports law, and even granting my request for a sabbatical leave to pursue my scholarly interest in sports law. I also am deeply indebted to the students at The University of Tulsa College of Law who have taken my sports law classes down through the years. They have helped to educate me and to convince me of the value of this kind of book. Many of them also good-naturedly agreed to pursue research topics I assigned rather than ones of their choosing in order to assist in the preparation of the book. I greatly appreciate that. Without my student research assistants, Jim Lammendola, Mary Beth (M. B.) Vasco, Jeff Tefelske, B. Wingo, and Bruce Almquist, the book would not have been completed prior to the USFL-NFL merger. I especially want to thank Bruce Almquist for his help in the final preparation of the manuscript. Greenwood editor Lynn Taylor will forever occupy a warm place in my heart—she saw the merit in what I was doing and was a moving force in securing a publication contract. Greenwood Production Editor Michelle Aucoin did a first-rate job in moving the manuscript through the production and publication phases. I would also like to thank my colleagues who supported my research effort in sports law. And I owe a great deal to Kay Hawkins, who typed, retyped, and typed again my numerous drafts. She was indispensable.

TORTS
AND
SPORTS

1

Tort Liability of One Participant to Another

Participation in sports carries with it special risks. It is probably fair to say that sports activities—playing baseball, basketball, football, tennis, and racketball, for example—create greater risks of physical harm than do most other human activities. Typically, injuries incurred in athletic competition are not of tortious origin. They occur as a result of the normal risks associated with participation in the sport. Thus, when a basketball player breaks his ankle after jumping and inadvertently landing on his opponent's foot, no lawyer worth his salt would be heard to argue that the opponent is a tortfeasor. In some instances, however, injuries occur as a consequence of arguably tortious behavior by a participant. This chapter explores those instances.

Generally, in an athletic event a participant who is injured by the act of another participant can base an action to recover on three theories. The first theory is an intentional tort theory, such as battery or assault. The second theory is negligence. The third theory available to the injured participant is based on recklessness.

A simple definition of battery is the intentional, unprivileged, harmful, or offensive contact by the defendant with the person of another. An assault is committed when the defendant, without privilege, intentionally places the plaintiff in apprehension of an immediate harmful or offensive touching. Sports activities are rife with what can arguably be termed assaults and batteries. A review of the cases indicates that the existence or nonexistence of a defense of privilege is often the key issue in such litigation. The Restatement provides the following definition of privilege.

§ 10. PRIVILEGE

(1) The word "privilege" is used . . . to denote the fact that conduct which, under ordinary circumstances, would subject the actor to liability, under particular circumstances does not subject him to such liability.

(2) A privilege may be based upon (a) the consent of the other affected by the actor's conduct, or (b) the fact that its exercise is necessary for the protection of some interest of the actor or of the public which is of such importance as to justify the harm caused or threatened by its exercise.

Privileges are thus categorized in terms of whether they are consensual or nonconsensual. Commonly accepted nonconsensual privileges include self-defense, defense of others, and defense of property. In sports, the consent privilege looms large. The courts are repeatedly faced with determining precisely what risks are consented to by a voluntary participant.

The basis of negligence as a cause of action is conduct which results in the creation of an unreasonable risk of harm to another. Recognize that almost all human activities involve some risk of harm. The gist of a negligence-based claim is that the conduct involves a risk of harm which is not outweighed by the benefits to be derived from engaging in the conduct. The Restatement states the generally applicable balancing test:

§ 291. UNREASONABLENESS: HOW DETERMINED: MAGNITUDE OF RISK AND UTILITY OF CONDUCT

Where an act is one which a reasonable man would recognize as involving a risk of harm to another, the risk is unreasonable and the act is negligent if the risk is of such magnitude as to outweigh what the law regards as the utility of the act or of the particular manner in which it is done.

When negligent conduct proximately causes harm, a prima facie case is made out. The main defenses to a negligence-based claim are contributory negligence and assumption of risk. (At common law each operated as a complete bar to the claim. Comparative negligence legislation now applicable in most states has changed this common law rule. Under comparative negligence statutes, a contributorily negligent plaintiff is not necessarily precluded from recovery.) A negligence-based claim in sports may well turn on the availability of the defense of assumption of risk. As with consent in the battery action, the assumption of risk defense will require the court to determine the nature of the risks that the willing participant assumes.

The third possible cause of action is recklessness. Recklessness is conduct which creates a higher degree of risk than that created by simple negligence. The Restatement states it thus:

§ 500. RECKLESS DISREGARD OF SAFETY DEFINED

The actor's conduct is in reckless disregard of the safety of another if he does an act or intentionally fails to do an act which it is his duty to the other to do, knowing or having reason to know of facts which would lead a reasonable man to realize, not only that his conduct creates an unreasonable risk of physical harm to another, but also that such risk is substantially greater than that which is necessary to make his conduct negligent.

Unlike the negligence cause of action, the plaintiff's contributory negligence does not operate as a defense to the defendant's reckless conduct. The defense of assumption of risk, however, may be a defense to the recklessness-based cause of action.

Finally, bear in mind that the issue of vicarious liability often arises in this context. An injured participant may want to look beyond the tortfeasor for a defendant to whom the tortfeasor's acts can properly be imputed. Typically, the most significant basis for imputing liability is the employer-employee relationship. Generally, torts committed by an employee within the scope of his employment may be imputed to the employer—who thus becomes vicariously liable for the damages caused. This principle is referred to as "respondeat superior"—literally, "let the master answer."

THE LANDMARK CASES

Bourque v. Duplechin
331 So. 2d 40 (La. Ct. App. 1976)

WATSON, Judge.
Plaintiff, Jerome Bourque, Jr., filed this suit to recover damages for personal injuries received in a softball game. . . . [The defendant was Adrien Duplechin, a member of the opposing team, who inflicted the injury. The trail court rendered judgment in favor of Bourque. Duplechin appealed.]

[Duplechin contends] . . . that the trial court erred; in not finding that Bourque assumed the risk of injury by participating in the softball game; and in failing to find that Bourque was guilty of contributory negligence. Defendant Duplechin also contends that the trial court erred in finding him negligent and in finding that the injury to plaintiff Bourque occurred four to five feet away from the second base position in the general direction of the pitcher's mound.

On June 9, 1974, Bourque was playing second base on a softball team fielded by Boo Boo's Lounge. Duplechin, a member of the opposing team sponsored by Murray's Steak House and Lounge, had hit the ball and advanced to first base. A teammate of Duplechin's, Steve Pressler, hit a ground ball and Duplechin started to second. The shortstop caught the ground ball and threw it to Bourque who tagged second base and then stepped away from second base to throw the ball to first and execute a double play. After Bourque had thrown the ball to first base, Duplechin ran at full speed into Bourque. As Duplechin ran into Bourque, he brought his left arm up under Bourque's chin. The evidence supports the trial court's factual conclusion that the collision occurred four or five feet away from the second base position in the direction of the pitcher's mound. Duplechin was thrown out of the game by the umpire because of the incident.

Pertinent to the trial court's decision was the following testimony:

Plaintiff Bourque, age 22 at the time of trial, testified that he is 5'7" tall. He was well out of the way when he was hit, standing four or five feet from second base and outside the base line. He knew there was a possibility of a runner sliding into him but had never imagined what actually happened, which he regarded as unbelievable under the circumstances.

Gregory John Laborde, a student at Tulane Law School, testified that he witnessed the incident from the dugout along the first base line and saw Duplechin turn and run directly toward Bourque who was standing four or five feet from second base toward home plate. Duplechin did not attempt to slide or decrease his speed and his left arm came up under Bourque's chin as they collided. Duplechin had to veer from the base path in order to strike Bourque.

Donald Frank Lockwood, baseball coach at USL, testified as an expert witness that: softball is a noncontact sport; in a forced play to second such as this, the accepted way to break up a double play is by sliding.

Steve Pressler, who hit the ground ball that precipitated the incident, testified that the sides were retired as a result, because the collision was a flagrant violation of the rules of the game.

Duplechin admitted that he ran into Bourque while standing up in an attempt to block Bourque's view of first base and keep him from executing a double play. Duplechin also admitted that he was running at full speed when he collided with Bourque, a much smaller man. Duplechin attributed the accident to Bourque's failure to get out of the way.

Oral surgeon John R. Wallace saw Bourque following the accident and said the nature of the injury and the x-rays indicated that it was caused by a blow from underneath the jaw. Dr. Wallace characterized the injury as one that may have been common in football before the use of mouthpieces and faceguards.

While other testimony was presented, both cumulative and contradictory, the evidence summarized above provides a reasonable evidentiary basis for the trial court's conclusions.

There is no question that defendant Duplechin's conduct was the cause in fact of the harm to plaintiff Bourque. Duplechin was under a duty to play softball in the ordinary fashion without unsportsmanlike conduct or wanton injury to his fellow players. This duty was breached by Duplechin, whose behavior was, according to the evidence, substandard and negligent. Bourque assumed the risk of being hit by a bat or a ball. [Citations omitted.] Bourque may also have assumed the risk of an injury resulting from standing in the base path and being spiked by someone sliding into second base, a common incident of softball and baseball. However, Bourque did not assume the risk of Duplechin going out of his way to run into him at full speed when Bourque was five feet away from the base. A participant in a game or sport assumes all of the risks incidental to that particular activity which are obvious and foreseeable. A participant does not assume the risk of injury from fellow players acting in an unexpected or unsportsmanlike way with a reckless lack of concern for others participating. [Citations omitted.] Assumption of risk is an affirmative defense which must be proven by a preponderance of the evidence, and the record here supports the trial court's conclusion that Bourque did not assume the risk of Duplechin's negligent act.

There is no evidence in the record to indicate contributory negligence on the part of Bourque.

. . . .

Duplechin was not motivated by a desire to injure Bourque. Duplechin tried to break up a double play with a reckless disregard of the consequences to Bourque. Duplechin's action was negligent but does not present a situation where the injury was expected or intended. . . .

The trial court awarded plaintiff Bourque $12,000 for his pain and suffering and $1,496.00 for his special damages. There is no dispute about the amount awarded. Bourque's jaw was fractured; his chin required plastic surgery; seven teeth were broken and had to be crowned; and one tooth was replaced by a bridge.

There is no manifest error in the trial court's conclusions which we summarize as follows: plaintiff Bourque's injuries resulted from the negligence of defendant Duplechin; Bourque was not guilty of contributory negligence and did not assume the risk of this particular accident. . . .

For the foregoing reasons, the judgment of the trial court is affirmed. . . .

AFFIRMED.

Nabozny v. Barnhill
31 Ill. App. 3d 212, 334 N.E.2d 258 (1975)

ADESKO, Justice.

Plaintiff, Julian Claudio Nabozny, a minor, by Edward J. Nabozny, his father, commenced this action to recover damages for personal injuries allegedly caused by the negligence of defendant, David Barnhill. Trial was before a jury. At the close of plaintiff's case on motion of defendant, the trial court directed a verdict in favor of the defendant. Plaintiff appeals from the order granting the motion.

Plaintiff contends on appeal that the trial judge erred in granting defendant's motion for a directed verdict and that plaintiff's actions as a participant do not prohibit the establishment of a prima facie case of negligence. Defendant argues in support of the trial court's ruling that defendant was free from negligence as a matter of law (lacking a duty to plaintiff) and that defendant was contributorily negligent as a matter of law.

. . . [O]ur statement of facts reflects an examination of all of the evidence viewed in its aspect most favorable to plaintiff.

A soccer match began between two amateur teams at Duke Child's Field in Winnetka, Illinois. Plaintiff was playing the position of goalkeeper for the Hansa team. Defendant was playing the position of forward for the Winnetka team. Members of both teams were of high-school age. Approximately twenty minutes after play had begun, a Winnetka player kicked the ball over the midfield line. Two players, Jim Gallos (for Hansa) and the defendant (for Winnetka), chased the free ball. Gallos reached the ball first. Since he was closely pursued by the defendant, Gallos passed the ball to the plaintiff, the Hansa goalkeeper. Gallos then turned away and prepared to receive a pass from the plaintiff. The plaintiff, in the meantime, went down on his left knee, received the pass, and pulled the ball to his chest. The defendant did not turn away when Gallos did, but continued to run in the direction of the plaintiff and kicked the left side of plaintiff's head causing plaintiff severe injuries.

All of the occurrence witnesses agreed that the defendant had time to avoid contact with plaintiff and that the plaintiff remained at all times within the "penalty area," a rectangular area between the eighteenth yard line and the goal. Four witnesses testified that they saw plaintiff in a crouched position on his left knee inside the penalty zone. Plaintiff testified that he actually had possession of the ball when he was struck by defendant. One witness, Marie Shekem, stated that plaintiff had the ball when he was kicked. All other occurrence witnesses stated that they thought plaintiff was in possession of the ball.

Plaintiff called three expert witnesses. Julius Roth, coach of the Hansa team, testified that the game in question was being played under "F.I.F.A." rules. The three experts agreed that those rules prohibited all players from making contact with the goalkeeper when he is in possession of the ball in the penalty area. Possession is defined in the Chicago area as referring to the goalkeeper having his hands on the ball. Under "F.I.F.A." rules, any contact with a goalkeeper in possession in the penalty area is an infraction of the rules, even if such contact is unintentional. The goalkeeper is the only member of a team who is allowed to touch a ball in play so long as he remains in the penalty area. The only legal contact permitted in soccer is shoulder to shoulder contact between players going for a ball within playing distance. The three experts agreed that the contact in question in this case should not have occurred. Additionally, goalkeeper head injuries are extremely rare in soccer. As a result of being struck, plaintiff suffered permanent damage to his skull and brain.

The initial question presented by this appeal is whether, under the facts in evidence, such a relationship existed between the parties that the court will impose a legal duty upon one for the benefit of the other. "[M]ore simply, whether the interest of the plaintiff which has suffered invasion was entitled to legal protection at the hands of the defendant." [Citation omitted.]

There is a dearth of case law involving organized athletic competition wherein one of the participants is charged with negligence. There are no such Illinois cases. A number of other jurisdictions prohibit recovery generally for reasons of public policy. [Citations omitted.] We can find no American cases dealing with the game of soccer.

This court believes that the law should not place unreasonable burdens on the free and vigorous participation in sports by our youth. However, we also believe that organized, athletic competition does not exist in a vacuum. Rather, some of the restraints of civilization must accompany every athlete onto the playing field. One of the educational benefits of organized athletic competition to our youth is the development of discipline and self control.

Individual sports are advanced and competition enhanced by a comprehensive set of rules. Some rules secure the better playing of the game as a test of skill. Other rules are primarily designed to protect participants from serious injury. [Citation omitted.]

For these reasons, this court believes that when athletes are engaged in an athletic competition, all teams involved are trained and coached by knowledgeable personnel; a recognized set of rules governs the conduct of the competition; and a safety rule is contained therein which is primarily designed to protect players from serious injury, a player is then charged with a legal duty to every other player on the field to refrain from conduct proscribed by a safety rule. A reckless disregard for

the safety of other players cannot be excused. To engage in such conduct is to create an intolerable and unreasonable risk of serious injury
to other participants. We have carefully drawn the rule announced herein
in order to control a new field of personal injury litigation. Under the
facts presented in the case at bar, we find such a duty clearly arose.
Plaintiff was entitled to legal protection at the hands of the defendant.
The defendant contends he is immune from tort action for any injury
to another player that happens during the course of a game, to which
theory we do not subscribe.

It is our opinion that a player is liable for injury in a tort action if his
conduct is such that it is either deliberate, wilful [sic] or with a reckless
disregard for the safety of the other player so as to cause injury to that
player, the same being a question of fact to be decided by a jury.

Defendant also asserts that plaintiff was contributorily negligent as a
matter of law, and, therefore, the trial court's direction of a verdict in
defendant's favor was correct. We do not agree. The evidence presented tended to show that plaintiff was in the exercise of ordinary care
for his own safety. While playing his position, he remained in the penalty area and took possession of the ball in a proper manner. Plaintiff
had no reason to know of the danger created by defendant. Without
this knowledge, it cannot be said that plaintiff unreasonably exposed
himself to such danger or failed to discover or appreciate the risk. The
facts in evidence revealed that the play in question was of a kind commonly executed in this sport. Frank Longo, one of the plaintiff's expert
witnesses, testified that once the goalkeeper gets possession of the ball
in the penalty area, "the instinct should be there . . . through training
and knowledge of the rules to avoid contact. . . . " All of plaintiff's
expert witnesses agreed that a player charging an opposition goal-
tender under circumstances similar to those which existed during the
play in question should be able to avoid all contact. Furthermore, it is
a violation of the rules for a player simply to kick at the ball when a
goalkeeper has possession in the penalty area even if no contact is made
with the goalkeeper.

. . . [W]e conclude that the trial court erred in directing a verdict in
favor of defendant. It is a fact question for the jury.

This cause, therefore, is reversed and remanded to the Circuit Court
of Cook County for a new trial consistent with the views expressed in
this opinion.

Reversed and remanded.

Hackbart v. Cincinnati Bengals, Inc. [*Hackbart I*]
435 F. Supp. 352 (D. Colo. 1977)

MATSCH, Judge.
Jurisdiction over this civil action is based upon diversity of citizen-

ship pursuant to 28 U.S.C. § 1332. By agreement of the parties, a separate trial to the court was held on the question of liability, with issues of damages and causation reserved. The case arises as a result of an incident which occurred in the course of a professional football game played between the Denver Broncos and the Cincinnati Bengals, in Denver, Colorado, on September 16, 1973.

The parties. The plaintiff, Dale Hackbart, is a citizen of Colorado who was a 35 year old contract player for the Denver Broncos Football Club in the National Football League at the time of the incident. He was then 6 feet 3 inches tall and weighed 210 pounds. Mr. Hackbart had 13 years' experience as a professional football player after competing in college and high school football, making a total of 21 years of experience in organized football.

The Denver game was the first regular season professional football game for the defendant, Charles Clark, who was then 23 years old with a weight of 240 pounds and a height of 6 feet 1-$^3/_4$ inches. Mr. Clark was a contract player for the Cincinnati Bengals Football Club, Inc., defendant herein, which was also a member of the National Football League. Both defendants are citizens of states other than Colorado.

The incident. The incident which gave rise to this lawsuit occurred near the end of the first half of the game at a time when the Denver team was leading by a score of 21 to 3. Dale Hackbart was playing a free safety position on the Broncos' defensive team and Charles Clark was playing fullback on the Bengals' offensive team. The Cincinnati team attempted to forward a pass play during which Charles Clark ran into a corner of the north end zone as a prospective receiver. That took him into an area which was the defensive responsibility of Mr. Hackbart. The thrown pass was intercepted near the goal line by a Denver linebacker who then began to run the ball upfield. The interception reversed the offensive and defensive roles of the two teams. As a result of an attempt to block Charles Clark in the end zone, Dale Hackbart fell to the ground. He then turned and, with one knee on the ground and the other leg extended, watched the play continue upfield. Acting out of anger and frustration, but without a specific intent to injure, Charles Clark stepped forward and struck a blow with his right forearm to the back of the kneeling plaintiff's head with sufficient force to cause both players to fall forward to the ground. Both players arose and, without comment, went to their respective teams along the sidelines. They both returned to play during the second half of the game.

Because no official observed it, no foul was called on the disputed play and Dale Hackbart made no report of this incident to his coaches or to anyone else during the game. Mr. Hackbart experienced pain and soreness to the extent that he was unable to play golf as he had planned on the day after the game, he did not seek any medical attention and, although he continued to feel pain, he played on specialty team assignments for the Denver Broncos in games against the Chicago Bears and the San Francisco Forty-Niners on successive Sundays. The Denver Broncos then released Mr. Hackbart on waivers and he was not claimed by any other team. After losing his employment, Mr. Hackbart sought medical assistance, at which time it was discovered that he had a neck injury. When that information was given to the Denver Broncos Football Club, Mr. Hackbart received his full payment for the 1973 season pursuant to an injury clause in his contract. . . .

Football is a recognized game which is widely played as a sport. Commonly, teams are organized by high schools and colleges and games are played according to rules provided by the association of such schools.

The basic design of the game is the same at the high school, college and professional levels. The differences are largely reflective of the fact that at each level the players have increased physical abilities, improved skills and differing motivations.

Football is a contest for territory. The objective of the offensive team is to move the ball through the defending team's area and across the vertical plane of the goal line. The defensive players seek to prevent that movement with their bodies. Each attempted movement involves collisions between the bodies of offensive and defensive players with considerable force and with differing areas of contact. The most obvious characteristic of the game is that all of the players engage in violent physical behavior.

The rules of play which govern the method and style by which the NFL teams compete include limitations on the manner in which players may strike or otherwise physically contact opposing players. During 1973, the rules were enforced by six officials on the playing field. The primary sanction for a violation was territorial with the amounts of yardage lost being dependent upon the particular infraction. Players were also subject to expulsion from the game and to monetary penalties imposed by the league commissioner.

The written rules are difficult to understand and, because of the speed and violence of the game, their application is often a matter of subjective evaluation of the circumstances. Officials differ with each other in their rulings. The players are not specifically instructed in the interpretation of the rules, and they acquire their working knowledge of them only from the actual experience of enforcement by the game officials during contests.

Many violations of the rules do occur during each game. Ordinarily each team receives several yardage penalties, but many fouls go undetected or undeclared by the officials.

Disabling injuries are also common occurrences in each contest. Hospitalization and surgery are frequently required for repairs. Protective clothing is worn by all players, but it is often inadequate to prevent bodily damage. Professional football players are conditioned to "play with pain" and they are expected to perform even though they are hurt. The standard player contract imposes an obligation to play when the club physician determines that an injured player has the requisite physical ability.

The violence of professional football is carefully orchestrated. Both offensive and defensive players must be extremely aggressive in their actions and they must play with a reckless abandonment of self-protective instincts. The coaches make studied and deliberate efforts to build the emotional levels of their players to what some call a "controlled rage."

John Ralston, the 1973 Broncos coach, testified that the pre-game psychological preparation should be designed to generate an emotion equivalent to that which would be experienced by a father whose family had been endangered by another driver who had attempted to force the family car off the edge of a mountain road. The precise pitch of motivation for the players at the beginning of the game should be the feeling of that father when, after overtaking and stopping the offending vehicle, he is about to open the door to take revenge upon the person of the other driver.

The large and noisy crowds in attendance at the games contribute to the emotional level of the players. Quick changes in the fortunes of the teams, the shock of violent collisions and the intensity of the competition make behavioral control extremely difficult, and it is not uncommon for players to "flare up" and begin fighting. The record made at this trial indicates that such incidents as that which gave rise to this action are not so unusual as to be unexpected in any NFL game.

The end product of all of the organization and effort involved in the professional football industry is an exhibition of highly developed individual skills in coordinated team competition for the benefit of large numbers of paying spectators, together with radio and television audiences. It is appropriate to infer that while some of those persons are attracted by the individual skills and precision performances of the teams, the appeal to others is the spectacle of savagery.

Plaintiff's theories of liability. This case is controlled by the law of Colorado. While a theory of intentional misconduct is barred by the applicable statute of limitations, the plaintiff contends that Charles Clark's foul was so far outside of the rules of plays and accepted practices of professional football that it should be characterized as reckless misconduct within the principles of Section 500 of the *Restatement of Torts, 2d.* A reckless disregard for the safety of a goalkeeper in a schoolboy soccer game was the basis for recovery in *Nabozny v. Barnhill*, 31 Ill. App. 3d 212, 334 N.E.2d 258 (1975).

Alternatively, the plaintiff claims that his injury was at least the result of a negligent act by the defendant. The difference in these contentions is but a difference in degree. Both theories are dependent upon a definition of a duty to the plaintiff and an objective standard of conduct based upon the hypothetical reasonably prudent person. Thus, the question is what would a reasonably prudent professional football player be expected to do under the circumstances confronting Charles Clark in this incident?

Two coaches testified at the trial of this case. Paul Brown has had 40 years of experience at all levels of organized football, with 20 years of coaching professional football. Both Mr. Brown and Mr. Ralston emphasized that the coaching and instructing of professional football players did not include any training with respect to a responsibility or even any regard for the safety of opposing players. They both said that aggressiveness was the primary attribute which they sought in the selection of players. Both emphasized the importance of emotional preparation of the teams. Mr. Brown said that flare-up fighting often occurred, even in practice sessions of his teams.

It is wholly incongruous to talk about a professional football player's duty of care for the safety of opposing players when he has been trained and motivated to be heedless of injury to himself. The character of NFL competition negates any notion that the playing conduct can be circumscribed by any standard of reasonableness.

Both theories of liability are also subject to the recognized defenses of consent and assumption of the risk. Here the question is what would a professional football player in the plaintiff's circumstances reasonably expect to encounter in a professional contest?

All of the witnesses with playing or coaching experience in the NFL agreed that players are urged to avoid penalties. The emphasis, however, is on the unfavorable effects of the loss of yardage, not the safety of the players. It is undisputed that no game is without penalties and that players frequently lose control in surges of emotion.

The conflict in the testimony is the difference in the witnesses' opinions as to whether Mr. Clark's act of striking the plaintiff on the back of the head in reaction to anger and frustration can be considered as "a part of the game." Several former players denounced this incident and said that Mr. Clark's conduct could not be considered customary or acceptable.

It is noteworthy that while this incident was clearly shown on the Denver Broncos' defensive game films, which were routinely reviewed by the defensive players and coaching staff, none of them made it a matter of special attention or concern.

Upon all of the evidence, my finding is that the level of violence and the frequency of emotional outbursts in NFL football games are such that Dale Hackbart must have recognized and accepted the risk that he would be injured by such an act as that committed by the defendant

Clark on September 16, 1973. Accordingly, the plaintiff must be held to have assumed the risk of such an occurrence. Therefore, even if the defendant breached a duty which he owed to the plaintiff, there can be no recovery because of assumption of the risk. . . .

Liability of the defendant Cincinnati Bengals, Inc. is based upon a contention that the Bengals failed to instruct and control their rookie fullback. The record, however, reflects that what he did is, unfortunately, an example of the excesses of violence which have become expectable as a result of the style of play in the NFL. The question of liability of the employer under the doctrine of respondeat superior is not presented because Charles Clark is not liable to the plaintiff.

The application of tort principles to professional football—a question of social policy. The business of the law of torts is to fix the dividing line between those cases in which a man is liable for harm which he has done, and those in which he is not. Justice O. W. Holmes, *The Common Law* (1881).

While the foregoing findings of fact and conclusions of law are determinative of the claim made by Dale Hackbart against Charles Clark and his employer, this case raises the larger question of whether playing field action in the business of professional football should become a subject for the business of the courts.

To compensate the injured at the expense of the wrongdoer, the courts have been compelled to construct principles of social policy. Through the processes of trial and error the judicial branch of government has historically evolved the common law principles which necessarily affect behavior in many contexts. The potential threat of liability for damages can have a significant deterrent effect and private civil actions are an important mechanism for societal control of human conduct. In recent years the pace of technical progress has accelerated and human conflicts have intensified. The resulting need to expand the body of governing law with greater rapidity and certainty than can be achieved through the litigation process has been met by legislation and administrative regulation. That is particularly true of industrial injuries. The coal mines became subject to the Federal Coal Mine Safety Act. The railroads have long been governed by the Federal Employers Liability Act and the Safety Appliance Act. The Occupational Health and Safety Act has broad application.

To this time professional football has been a self-regulated industry. The only protection which NFL contract players have beyond self-defense and real or threatened retaliation is that which is provided by the league rules and sanctions. It may well be true that what has been provided is inadequate and that these young athletes have been exploited and subjected to risks which should be unacceptable in our social order. In this respect, it is interesting to compare football with boxing.

Because of the essential brutality of the contest, prize fighting has been held to be unlawful unless conducted under the sanction and authority of a governmental commission. [Citation and footnote omitted.]

Football has been presumed to be lawful and, indeed, professional football has received the implicit approval of government because these contests take place in arenas owned by local governments and the revenues are subject to taxation. Like coal mining and railroading, professional football is hazardous to the health and welfare of those who are employed as players.

What is the interest of the larger community in limiting the violence of professional football? That question concerns not only the protection of the participants, but also the effects of such violence on those who observe it. Can the courts answer this question? I think not. An ordinary citizen is entitled to protection according to the usages of the society in which he lives, and in the context of common community standards there can be no question but that Mr. Clark's blow here would generate civil liability. It would involve a criminal sanction if the requisite intent were present. The difference here is that this blow was delivered on the field of play during the course of action in a regularly scheduled professional football game. The Illinois court was concerned with the safety of high school athletes in *Nabozny v. Barnhill*, at 215, 334 N.E.2d at 260 and said: "This court believes that the law should not place unreasonable burdens on the free and vigorous participation in sports by our youth. However, we also believe that organized, athletic competition does not exist in a vacuum. Rather, some of the restraints of civilization must accompany every athlete onto the playing field. One of the educational benefits of organized athletic competition to our youth is the development of discipline and self control."

The difficulty with that view as applied to professional football is that to decide which restraints should be made applicable is a task for which the courts are not well suited. There is no discernible code of conduct for NFL players. The dictionary definition of a sportsman is one who abides by the rules of a contest and accepts victory or defeat graciously. *Webster's Third New International Dictionary*, p. 2206 (1971). That is not the prevalent attitude in professional football. There are no Athenian virtues in this form of athletics. The NFL has substituted the morality of the battlefield for that of the playing field, and the "restraints of civilization" have been left on the sidelines.

Mr. Justice Holmes' simple statement of the function of tort law and the evidentiary record now before me clearly reveal the density of the thicket in which the courts would become entangled if they undertook the task of allocation of fault in professional football games. The NFL rules of play are so legalistic in their statement and so difficult of application because of the speed and violence of the play that the differences between violations which could fairly be called deliberate, reckless or outrageous and those which are "fair play" would be so small and subjective as to be incapable of articulation. The question of causation would be extremely difficult in view of the frequency of forceful collisions. The volume of such litigation would be enormous and it is reasonable to expect that the court systems of the many states in which NFL games are played would develop differing and conflicting principles of law. It is highly unlikely that the NFL could continue to produce anything like the present games under such multiple systems of overview by judges and juries. If there is to be any governmental involvement in this industry, it is a matter which can be best considered by the legislative branch.

My conclusion that the civil courts cannot be expected to control the violence in professional football is limited by the facts of the case before me. I have considered only a claim for an injury resulting from a blow, without weaponry, delivered emotionally without a specific intent to injure, in the course of regular play in a league-approved game involving adult, contract players. Football as a commercial enterprise is something quite different from athletics as an extension of the academic experience and what I have said here may have no applicability in other areas of physical competition.

Upon the foregoing findings of fact and conclusions of law, it is

ORDERED that judgment shall enter for the defendants, with costs to be taxed.

Hackbart v. Cincinnati Bengals, Inc. [*Hackbart II*]
601 F.2d 516 (10th Cir. 1979)

WILLIAM E. DOYLE, Circuit Judge.

The question in this case is whether in a regular season professional football game an injury which is inflicted by one professional football player on an opposing player can give rise to liability in tort where the injury was inflicted by the intentional striking of a blow during the game. . . .

The judge resolved the liability issue in favor of the Cincinnati team and Charles Clark. Consistent with this result, final judgment was entered for Cincinnati and the appeal challenges this judgment. In essence the trial court's reasons for rejecting plaintiff's claim were that professional football is a species of warfare and that so much physical force is tolerated and the magnitude of the force exerted is so great that it renders injuries not actionable in court; that even intentional batteries are beyond the scope of the judicial process. . . .

The evidence at the trial uniformly supported the proposition that the intentional striking of a player in the head from the rear is not an accepted part of either the playing rules or the general customs of the game of professional football. The trial court, however, believed that the unusual nature of the case called for the consideration of underlying policy which it defined as common law principles which have evolved as a result of the case to case process and which necessarily affect behavior in various contexts. From these considerations the belief was expressed that even *intentional* injuries incurred in football games should be outside the framework of the law. The court recognized that the potential threat of legal liability has a significant deterrent effect, and further said that private civil actions constitute an important mechanism for societal control of human conduct. Due to the increase in severity of human conflicts, a need existed to expand the body of governing law more rapidly and with more certainty, but that this had to be accomplished by legislation and administrative regulation. The judge compared football to coal mining and railroading insofar as all are inherently hazardous. Judge Matsch said that in the case of football it was questionable whether social values would be improved by limiting the violence.

Thus the district court's assumption was that Clark had inflicted an intentional blow which would ordinarily generate civil liability and which might bring about a criminal sanction as well, but that since it had occurred in the course of a football game, it should not be subject to the restraints of the law; that if it were it would place unreasonable impediments and restraints on the activity. The judge also pointed out that courts are ill-suited to decide the different social questions and to administer conflicts on what is much like a battlefield where the restraints of civilization have been left on the sidelines.

We are forced to conclude that the result reached is not supported by evidence.

Plaintiff, of course, maintains that tort law applicable to the injury in this case applies on the football field as well as in other places. On the other hand, plaintiff does not rely on the theory of negligence being applicable. This is in recognition of the fact that subjecting another to unreasonable risk of harm, the essence of negligence, is inherent in the game of football, for admittedly it is violent. Plaintiff maintains that in the area of contributory fault, a vacuum exists in relationship to intentional infliction of injury. Since negligence does not apply, contributory negligence is inapplicable. Intentional or reckless contributory fault could theoretically at least apply to infliction of injuries in reckless disregard of the rights of others. This has some similarity to contributory negligence and undoubtedly it would apply if the evidence would justify it. But it is highly questionable whether a professional football player consents or submits to injuries caused by conduct not within the rules, and there is no evidence which we have seen which shows this. However, the trial court did not consider this question and we are not deciding it.

Contrary to the position of the court then, there are no principles of law which allow a court to rule out certain tortious conduct by reason of general roughness of the game or difficulty of administering it.

Indeed, the evidence shows that there are rules of the game which prohibit the intentional striking of blows. Thus, Article 1, Item 1, Subsection C, provides that: "All players are prohibited from striking on the head, face or neck with the heel, back or side of the hand, wrist, forearm, elbow or clasped hands." Thus the very conduct which was present here is expressly prohibited by the rule which is quoted above.

The general customs of football do not approve the intentional punching or striking of others. That this is prohibited was supported by the testimony of all of the witnesses. They testified that the intentional striking of a player in the face or from the rear is prohibited by the playing rules as well as the general customs of the game. Punching or hitting with the arms is prohibited. Undoubtedly these restraints are intended to establish reasonable boundaries so that one football player cannot intentionally inflict a serious injury on another. Therefore, the notion is not correct that all reason has been abandoned, whereby the only possible remedy for the person who has been the victim of an unlawful blow is retaliation. . . .

The Restatement of Torts Second, § 500, distinguishes between reckless and negligent misconduct. Reckless misconduct differs from negligence, according to the authors, in that negligence consists of mere inadvertence, lack of skillfulness or failure to take precautions; reckless misconduct, on the other hand, involves a choice or adoption of a course of action either with knowledge of the danger or with knowledge of facts which would disclose this danger to a reasonable man. Recklessness also differs in that it consists of intentionally doing an act with knowledge not only that it contains a risk of harm to others as does negligence, but that it actually involves a risk substantially greater in magnitude than is necessary in the case of negligence. The authors explain the difference, therefore, in the degree of risk by saying that the difference is so significant as to amount to a difference in kind.

Subsection (f) also distinguishes between reckless misconduct and intentional wrongdoing. To be reckless the *act* must have been intended by the actor. At the same time, the actor does not intend to cause the harm which results from it. It is enough that he realized, or from the facts should have realized, that there was a strong probability that harm would result even though he may hope or expect that this conduct will prove harmless. Nevertheless, existence of probability is different from substantial certainty which is an ingredient of intent to cause the harm which results from the act.

Therefore, recklessness exists where a person knows that the act is harmful but fails to realize that it will produce the extreme harm which it did produce. It is in this respect that recklessness and intentional conduct differ in degree.

In the case at bar the defendant Clark admittedly acted impulsively and in the heat of anger, and even though it could be said from the admitted facts that he intended the act, it could also be said that he did not intend to inflict serious injury which resulted from the blow which he struck.

In ruling that recklessness is the appropriate standard and that assault and battery is not the exclusive one, we are saying that these two liability concepts are not necessarily opposed one to the other. Rather, recklessness under § 500 of the Restatement might be regarded, for the purpose of analysis at least, a lesser included act.

Assault and battery, having originated in a common law writ, is narrower than recklessness in its scope. In essence, two definitions enter into it. The assault is an attempt coupled with the present ability to commit a violent harm against another. Battery is the unprivileged or unlawful touching of another. Assault and battery then call for an intent, as does recklessness. But in recklessness the intent is to do the act, but without an intent to cause the particular harm. It is enough if the actor knows that there is a strong probability that harm will result. Thus, the definition fits perfectly the fact situation here. Surely, then, no reason exists to compel appellant to employ the assault and battery standard which does not comfortably apply fully in preference to the standard which meets this fact situation.

· · · · · · · ·

In sum, having concluded that the trial court did not limit the case to a trial of the evidence bearing on defendant's liability but rather determined that as a matter of social policy the game was so violent and unlawful that valid lines could not be drawn, we take the view that this was not a proper issue for determination and that plaintiff was entitled to have the case tried on an assessment of his rights and whether they had been violated.

The trial court has heard the evidence and has made findings. The findings of fact based on the evidence presented are not an issue on this appeal. Thus, it would not seem that the court would have to repeat the areas of evidence that have already been fully considered. The need is for a reconsideration of that evidence in the light of that which is taken up by this court in its opinion. We are not to be understood as limiting the trial court's consideration of supplemental evidence if it deems it necessary. . . .

A CASE STUDY—*TOMJANOVICH v. CALIFORNIA SPORTS, INC.*

The plaintiff in the case is Rudy Tomjanovich, a veteran professional basketball player, employed by the Houston Rockets, Inc., a professional basketball franchise based in Houston, Texas. The defendant is California Sports, Inc., which does business as the Los Angeles Lakers, a professional basketball team. The plaintiff's cause of action arose out of an altercation that took place during a basketball game between the Lakers and the Rockets. During the course of the game Tomjanovich was punched in the face by Kermit Washington, a Los Angeles Lakers' player.

The undisputed facts reveal that the incident began with a fight between Kermit Washington and another Rockets' player, Kevin Kunnert. A film of the incident showed that Washington grabbed Kunnert, and blows were exchanged. Tomjanovich then approached, and Washington punched him in the face with enough force to leave Tomjanovich with a fractured skull, nose, and jaw, a brain concussion, facial lacerations, leakage of spinal fluid, and other serious complications.

The plaintiff offered a number of theories to support a cause of action against the Lakers. He alleged that Kermit Washington's attack was tortious and that the Lakers were vicariously liable for Washington's torts. The plaintiff contended that Washington was negligent, reckless, and guilty of intentional wrongdoing. He asserted that no matter how Washington's tort was characterized, the Lakers were vicariously liable under the theory of respondeat superior. Tomjanovich also alleged that the Lakers were themselves negligent in their supervision of Washington. In this regard, the plaintiff claimed that the Lakers failed to control, train, and discipline Washington. Punitive damages were requested for all causes of action.

Along with a general denial, the Lakers alleged, by way of affirmative defense, that insofar as the negligence-based cause of action was concerned, Tomjanovich was contributorily negligent and assumed the risk. They further alleged that the recklessness-based cause of action was barred by Tomjanovich's reckless indifference to his own welfare and that the battery cause of action was defeated by the privileges of consent and self-defense.

The trial lasted 10 days, during which time the plaintiff and defendant introduced testimony from eyewitnesses and experts, and the jury reviewed films and photographs of the events surrounding the occurrence. What follows is the gist of what was established by the massive amount of evidence.

The plaintiff's evidence tended to establish that Tomjanovich was acting as a peacemaker when he approached Washington and Kunnert, who were scuffling. Tomjanovich appeared to be unprepared for the punch which floored him and was unable to defend himself from the blow. It appeared that he ran right into the punch. It was the kind of blow that was unexpected in professional basketball; it was not customary and was excessive. Testimony was received concerning the vicious nature of the blow, with Kareem Abdul-Jabbar summing it up best by saying that, when he heard the impact of the punch, he thought that it sounded "like a watermelon being dropped on a cement floor." The plaintiff also offered evidence establishing the extensive damage caused by the blow. Evidence of the defendant's wealth was received as relevant to the issue of punitive damages. On the negligent supervision cause of action, Tomjanovich introduced evidence showing that the Lakers in fact encouraged overly aggressive play, that they did not discipline and, in fact, paid the fines for players penalized for such play, that they encouraged Washington to be featured in a *Sports Illustrated* article on basketball's "enforcers," and that, subsequent to the Washington-Tomjanovich incident, they "ratified" Washington's conduct by paying his league imposed fine and by not disciplining him.

The defendant's evidence tended to show that professional basketball was an inherently "physical" game in which fights and scuffles were foreseeable. The Lakers' version of the incident was designed to show that Tomjanovich did not act reasonably in protecting himself, that he knew or should have known of the risks, and that Washington reasonably believed he was in danger when he glimpsed Tomjanovich approaching him rapidly. The Lakers presented evidence that they were indeed attempting to deal with the problem of on-court violence, and they threatened overly aggressive players with the loss of playing time and even with the loss of their spot on the roster, but that to a certain extent violence in pro basketball was to be expected because, to a limited extent, it was an intrinsic part of the game.

How is the case likely to be resolved? Why?

Discussion

The negligence-based cause of action. Although *Bourque* indicates that a negligence-based cause of action is appropriate in this setting, the trend is away from the negligence claim. In fact, *Bourque* suggests as much when the court points out that the sports participant assumes "all risks incidental to that particular activity which are obvious and foreseeable" but does not assume "the risk of injury from fellow players acting in an unexpected or unsportsmanlike way with a reckless lack of concern for others participating." The thrust of *Bourque* is that the simple negligence cause of action will in almost all cases be defeated by the assumption-of-risk defense. In short, the sports participant invariably assumes the risks created by the coparticipant's negligence but does not necessarily assume those risks created by the coparticipant's reckless-ness. *Bourque* is really more accurately viewed as a case in which the defendant was liable because he was reckless and not because he was negligent.

Nabozny and both *Hackbart I* and *Hackbart II* also suggest that the sim-ple negligence claim is doomed to failure. Although negligence was pleaded in *Nabozny*, the court opinion stressed that "a player is liable if his conduct is such that it is either deliberate, wilful or with a reck-less disregard for the safety of the other player." The negative impli-cation of *Nabozny* is that simple negligence will not do. The plaintiff in *Hackbart* did not even rely on a negligence theory. As the *Hackbart II* court pointed out, "This [was] in recognition of the fact that subjecting another to unreasonable risk of harm, the essence of negligence, is in-herent in the game of football."

Still, a lawyer pleading a case arising out of a playing-field incident ought to plead the negligence-based cause of action simply because the ground rules in such cases have not been clearly identified. The best advice to a practitioner representing an injured sports participant is to plead the three causes of action in the alternative. (This would be done in the same manner as one would plead breach of warranty, negli-gence, and strict liability on behalf of a consumer injured by a defective product.) The informed practitioner ought to recognize that the negli-gence-based claim is probably a loser.

The recklessness and intentional tort causes of action. The relevant case law now clearly supports the view that an injured sports participant can recover upon a showing of recklessness or intention. The sugges-tion in *Hackbart I* that the sports participant is insulated from tort lia-bility has been almost universally discredited. *Hackbart II* reflects the modern view that both recklessness and battery are the appropriate causes of action.

The key to the litigation might often turn on the availability of the defenses. In the recklessness context, the primary defense is akin to as-sumption of risk. It is interesting to note, however, that other defenses to a recklessness-based cause of action have not been clearly deline-ated. As *Hackbart II* notes, the distinctions between recklessness and negligence and between recklessness and intention are not bright-line. As Oliver Wendell Holmes noted:

If the manifest probability of harm is very great . . . we say that it is done intentionally; if not so great but still considerable, we say that the harm is done negligently; if there is no apparent danger, we call it mischance. O. W. Holmes, "Privilege, Malice, and Intent," 8 HARV. L. REV. 1 (1894).

As far as recklessness is concerned, we might say that if the manifest probability of harm is not very great but quite considerable, we call it recklessness. Because the distinctions are not altogether clear, and because recklessness has only recently emerged as a separate and distinct cause of action, the available defenses to the recklessness claim have not been clearly articulated. In light of the uncertainty, a practitioner would be well advised to plead the well-established intentional tort defenses of consent, self-defense, defense of others, and defense of property along with the well-established negligence defenses of assumption of risk and contributory negligence and let the court sort it all out.

The intentional tort theory would of course be much more cut-and-dried, and, as previously noted, the available defenses are well-established and generally agreed upon. In the sports context, self-defense, defense of others, and consent are most often relevant.

A brief note on vicarious liability. There is uniform agreement that the negligence of an employee committed during the scope of employment is properly imputed to the employer. A recurring question, however, is whether intentional torts are properly viewed as being within the scope of employment. The common law rule was that such wrongs were not within the scope of employment. The modern trend is that intentional torts can be regarded as being within the scope of employment if it can be shown that the act was closely connected to the employment. There is still considerable split of authority on this issue, and the lawyer must be familiar with the case law from the appropriate jurisdiction. (See Brill, The Liability of an Employer for the Wilful Torts of His Servants, 45 CHI.[-]KENT L. REV. 1 (1968); Note, Respondeat Superior and the Intentional Tort: A Short Discourse on How to Make Assault and Battery a Part of the Job, 45 U. CIN. L. REV. 235 (1976).) Similar problems arise in regard to torts grounded upon recklessness.

Negligent supervision. It should also be remembered that employers might be liable because of their own tortious conduct, as distinguished from the tortious conduct of their employees. Recall that in *Hackbart*, one of the plaintiff's theories was that the Bengals were responsible for the harm because of their negligence in instructing and controlling their rookie fullback. Tomjanovich clearly pleaded, and attempted to prove, negligent supervision. This is a newly emerging but increasingly viable cause of action. The thrust of the action is that the employer created unreasonable risks of harm by acting in such a way as to create an atmosphere in which the players believed that violence was an acceptable, if not a desirable, mechanism to ensure winning. Recall here Coach Ralston's testimony in *Hackbart I* that he prepares his players by asking them to assume the mind-set of a father whose family's safety is threatened. This kind of training would appear to create unreasonable risks of harm.

Availability of Punitive Damages

In *Sebastian v. Wood*, 246 Iowa 94, 100–1, 66 N.W.2d 841, 844–45, the Iowa Supreme Court articulated the rationale for permitting punitive damage awards:

[The] main purpose [of punitive damages] as indicated in their designation is that they are awarded under proper circumstances and conditions as a punishment for the particular party involved and as a warning and an example to him in the future, and to all others who may offend in like manner. The award of such damages constitutes an effective deterrent to such offenders, and a salutary protection to society and the public in general. They are not recoverable as a matter of right and are only incidental to the main cause of action, and can be awarded only when actual and substantial damages are allowed. They are in no way compensatory, and while they have a secondary purpose in addition to the complainant's award because injury to him may well have been aggravated by its malicious, oppressive, willful, wanton, or reckless causation, yet, whatever benefit he so receives comes to him not as compensation for the wrong done him but as purely incidental and by the grace and gratuity of the law, as punishment of the wrongdoer, and as an example and deterrent to others. The opinions of this court have always emphasized the thought that the purpose of exemplary damages was the punishment, and prevention of similar future offenses. The allowance of such damages is wholly within the function and province of the jury, to be granted or denied in the exercise of a wise discretion, whether the moving cause be effected by malice, oppression, wantonness, recklessness, or gross negligence, and, if allowed, to fix the amount.

Ordinarily punitive damages are available only if the conduct can be characterized as something worse than negligence. Again, you must consult your local jurisdiction for more specific guidance.

A related issue is whether the employer can be held liable for punitive damages in a case where the liability is established under principles of respondeat superior. Some states allow punitive damages without any showing of particular wrongdoing on the part of the employer. Other states require a showing of an intentional act or authorization or ratification on the part of the employer. (See generally Note, Liability of Employers for Punitive Damages Resulting from Acts of Employees, 54 CHI.[-] KENT L. REV. 829 (1978).) And finally, whether punitive damages are appropriate in a case grounded on negligent supervision is problematical. As already noted, something worse than ordinary negligence is a necessary prerequisite for punitive damages. But an argument could be made that negligent supervision, which creates the risk that the employee will act recklessly or with intent to injure, justifies the imposition of punitive damages.

Tomjanovich v. California Sports, Inc.—The Actual Outcome

A federal jury found that Washington was liable to Tomjanovich for a battery. The jury rejected Washington's self-defense argument. It also found that the Lakers were liable. See 23 ATLA L. REP. at 107 for its account of the celebrated case, *Rudy Tomjanovich v. California Sports, Inc.*. The jury's award was for $3.2 million (of which $1.5 million was for punitive damages). A remittitur was ordered for a portion of the future medical expenses, and judgment was entered for the plaintiff for a total of $3.1 million.

ADDITIONAL NOTES

1. It should be noted that the *Tomjanovich* litigation also included a claim by the Houston Rockets that the Lakers intentionally interfered with the contractual relations of the Rockets and Tomjanovich. Following Tomjanovich's favorable verdict, the Rockets and Lakers settled this claim for approximately $750,000 to compensate the Rockets for loss of Tomjanovich's services, gate receipts, and money spent replacing Tomjanovich.

2. One final note on *Tomjanovich* concerns the issue of employer "ratification." Tomjanovich contended, in regard to his negligent supervision claim, that the Lakers ratified Washington's conduct by their failure to reprimand him and by their paying the fine subsequently levied by the league against Washington. The court subsequently instructed the jury that it could award punitive damages on the negligent supervision claim if it found that the Lakers had indeed ratified Washington's malicious act. The jury, in turn, apparently did award punitive damages on this basis.

3. If "participant" is defined broadly, it could include referees, cheerleaders, and coaches. Although the general rules of liability remain unchanged, the problems raised by these participants are unique.

A tort case against a referee might well involve a theory of negligent supervision. For example, a referee who permits a boxing match to continue when a reasonable referee would stop the fight might be named as a defendant in a lawsuit by the injured boxer. On the other hand, a referee attacked by a disgruntled participant might think of initiating a lawsuit of his own on a battery theory.

Cheerleaders can be viewed as participants in their own sporting event, which takes place within the confines of the "main" competition. Thus, a cheerleader who is injured when performing an acrobatic cheer may well be the victim of a tortfeasor-coparticipant. Recently, attention is being paid to human pyramids, featuring dramatic blind falls as a climax. A negligence-based cause of action might be available to an injured cheerleader against the cheerleading coach who instructed the squad to build such a pyramid.

The liability of coaches deserves special attention. In a negligence-based action, the issue will be whether the coach fulfilled the duty to use reasonable care for the protection of the athletes. In a series of reported cases, coaches have been deemed to have fallen below that standard. Liability has been imposed, for example, when a coach plays an injured player, *Morris v. Union High School Dist. A, King County*, 160 Wash. 121, 194 P. 998 (1931); fails to properly direct the movement of an injured player, *Welch v. Dunsmuir Joint Union School Dist.*, 326 P.2d 633 (Cal. Dist. Ct. App. 1958); fails to promptly acquire medical attention for heat stroke, *Mogabgab v. Orleans Parish School Bd.*, 239 So.2d 456 (La. App. 1970); and fails to adequately instruct on safe techniques for participation, *Stehn v. Bernarr McFadden Foundations, Inc.*, 434 F.2d 811 (6th Cir. 1970). It is not difficult to imagine other contexts in which a coach might be liable for an injury to a player. The celebrated Frank Kush–Kevin Rutledge incident—in which Coach Kush grabbed and shook the facemask of his erring punter—indicates that sometimes overzealous, physical "coaching" takes on tortious dimensions. Here we would be talking about liability for an intentional tort rather than negligence. Situations in which a coach defames a player or invades a player's privacy by publicly disclosing private facts are by no means unforeseeable. The point to be made is that, perhaps because of the nature of the player-coach relationship, coaches often find themselves on the receiving end of players' lawsuits. A partial list of these cases can be found in Weistart and Lowell, pp. 980–982.

4. In *Murphy v. Steeplechase Amusement Company, Inc.*, 250 N.Y. 479, 482, 166 N.E. 173, 174 (1929), Judge Cardozo stated: "One who takes part in . . . a sport accepts the dangers that inhere in it so far as they are obvious and necessary." Is this helpful? What dangers are "obvious and necessary" to a professional hockey player? to a professional football player? to a college football player? to a Little League baseball player?

In "the fireman's chair" case, *Arnold v. Schmeiser* 34 A.D.2d 568, 309 N.Y.S.2d 699 (1970), it was held that the plaintiff assumed the risk that his fellow participants would fail to catch him when they tossed him in the air but that he did not assume the risk that his fellow participants would *refuse* to catch him. The case is an apt metaphor of the nature of the risks assumed.

5. Arguably, the following fairly common situations present tort cases:

(a) the "brushback" pitch;

(b) the response to the brushback, wherein the batter runs toward the pitcher and punches him or strikes him with the bat;

(c) the Billy Martin–Earl Weaver-type tantrum, in which the umpire has dirt kicked upon him or tobacco juice sprayed in his face;

(d) the "spikes-up" slide;

(e) the "cheap-shot" in football, where a player is hit either out-of-bounds or after the whistle;

(f) the "clean but brutal" hit, where the tackler intends to cripple a vulnerable opponent, à la Jack Tatum–Daryl Stingley;

(g) the "low bridge" in basketball, where the perpetrator runs under the airborne opponent;

(h) the "gloves off" hockey fight.

6. One point is clear. The sports participant does not enjoy talismanic immunity from tort liability, the comments of Judge Matsch in *Hackbart I* to the contrary notwithstanding. The obvious goal of any practitioner is to distinguish those cases that have a reasonable chance for success from those that do not. The materials in this chapter are, ultimately, designed to assist the practitioner in drawing that distinction. It does appear, however, that sports activity is one area of human behavior where the participants are indeed insulated from liability for ordinary negligence. Perhaps this is one thing that makes sports a special and unique form of human experience—participants are free to be unreasonable (but not reckless).

BIBLIOGRAPHY

"Amusements and Exhibitions: Injuries to Participants in Games, or Amusement or Sports Activities," 4 American Jurisprudence 2d 226, § 98 (1962).

"Amusements and Exhibitions: Liability of Participant in Game or Sport," 4 American Jurisprudence 2d 210, § 86 (1962).

"Assault and Battery—Liability for Injuries Received in Athletic Contests," 26 MICHIGAN LAW REVIEW 322 (1927).

"Assumption of Risk and Vicarious Liability in Personal Injury Actions Brought by Professional Athletes," 1980 DUKE LAW JOURNAL 742.

Blumler, Candyce, "Liability in Professional Sports: An Alternative to Violence?" 22 ARIZONA LAW REVIEW 919 (1980).

"The 'Booby' Trap: Does the Violent Nature of Professional Football Vitiate the Doctrine of Due Care in Participant Tort Litigation?: *Hackbart v. Cincinnati Bengals, Inc.*, 435 F. Supp. 352 (D. Colo. 1977)," 10 CONNECTICUT LAW REVIEW 365 (1978).

"Compensating Injured Professional Athletes: The Mystique of Sport Versus Traditional Tort Principles," 55 NEW YORK UNIVERSITY LAW REVIEW 971 (1980).

"Federal Jurisdiction—Torts—Federal District Court in Diversity Suit May Not Refuse Jurisdiction Over Professional Football Player's Claim for Damages Resulting from Blow Intentionally Inflicted, *Hackbart v. Cincinnati Bengals, Inc.*, 601 F.2d 516 (10 Cir.) *cert. denied*, 100 S. Ct. 275 (1979)," 11 RUTGERS-CAMDEN LAW JOURNAL 497 (1980).

"Injuries to Participants in Sporting Events," 65A Corpus Juris Secundum 302 § 174(6), (1966).

"Judicial Scrutiny of Tortious Conduct in Professional Sports: Do Professional Athletes Assume the Risk of Injuries Resulting from Rule Violations? *Hackbart v. Cincinnati Bengals, Inc.*," 17 CALIFORNIA WESTERN LAW REVIEW 149 (1980).

Lambert, Dale J., "Tort Law and Participant Sports: The Line Between Vigor and Violence," 4 JOURNAL OF CONTEMPORARY LAW 211 (1978).

"Liability for Injury to or Death of a Participant in Game or Contest," 7 American Law Reports 2d 704 (1949).

Moore, Charles C., "Civil or Criminal Liability for Injuries in Field Sports," 19 CASE & COMMENT 163 (1912).

"Negligence—Illustrative Applications; Sports, Games and Contests," 57 American Jurisprudence 2d 678 § 284 (1971).

"On Finding Civil Liability Between Professional Football Players: *Hackbart v. Cincinnati Bengals, Inc.*," 15 NEW ENGLAND LAW REVIEW 741 (1980).

"Participant's Liability for Injury to a Fellow Participant in an Organized Athletic Event," 53 CHICAGO[-]KENT LAW REVIEW 97 (1976).

Peterson, Terri L., "Sports Injury Litigation: The Role of the Lawyer on the Playing Field," 7 BARRISTER 10 (Summer 1980).

"Professional Football Player Intentionally Strikes Opponent Outside Rules of the Game and Is Liable Under Recklessness Standard," 23 AMERICAN TRIAL LAWYERS ASSOCIATION LAW REPORTER 108 (1980).

"Professional Sports and Tort Liability: A Victory for the Intentionally Injured Player," 1980 DETROIT COLLEGE OF LAW REVIEW 687 (1980).

"Sports Injury—Intentional Acts," 18 AMERICAN JURISPRUDENCE PROOF OF FACTS 2d (1970).

"Sports Participant in Athletic Contest States Cause of Action for Injuries, Intentionally or Recklessly Inflicted by Opposing Player," 23 AMERICAN TRIAL LAWYERS ASSOCIATION LAW REPORTER 108 (1980).

"Tort Law—Reckless Misconduct in Sports," 19 DUQUESNE LAW REVIEW 191 (1980).

"Tort Liability for Players in Contact Sports: *Nabozny v. Barnhill*," 45 UNIVERSITY OF MISSOURI AT KANSAS CITY LAW REVIEW 119 (1976).

"Tort Liability in Professional Sports: Battle in the Sports Arena, *Hackbart v. Cincinnati Bengals, Inc.*, 435 F. Supp. 352 (D. Colo. 1977)," 57 NEBRASKA LAW REVIEW 1128 (1978).

"Torts—Assumption of Risk—A Professional Football Player Assumes the Risk of Receiving a Blow, Delivered Out of Anger and Frustration, but without Specific Intention to Injure, During a Game," 12 GEORGIA LAW REVIEW 380 (1978).

"Torts—Civil Liability of Athletes—Professional Football Player May Have Tort Claim for Injuries Intentionally Inflicted During Football Game. *Hackbart v. Cincinnati Bengals, Inc.*, 601 F.2d 516 (10th Cir. 1979)," 84 DICKINSON LAW REVIEW 753 (1980).

"Torts and Sports," 23 AMERICAN TRIAL LAWYERS ASSOCIATION LAW
    REPORTER 107 (1980).
"Torts in Sports—Deterring Violence in Professional Athletics," 48 FORDHAM
    LAW REVIEW 764 (1980).
"Torts—Participant in Athletic Competition States Cause of Action for Injuries
    Against Other Participants: *Nabozny v. Barnhill*," 42 MISSOURI LAW RE-
    VIEW 347 (1977).
Turro, Andrew J., "Tort Liability in Professional Sports," 44 ALBANY LAW
    REVIEW 696 (1980).
Zupance, Donald M., "Liability of Participant in Team Athletic Competition for
    Injury to or Death of Another Participant," 77 American Law Reports 3d
    1300 (1977).

2

The Spectator as Plaintiff

Spectators at sporting events are exposed to special risks. Racing cars occasionally hurtle over barriers and injure spectators. Foul balls, errant pucks, and misplayed golf balls strike spectators with some regularity. Spectators injure one another in their quest for souvenirs. On occasion, the spectator-heckler is injured by the short-tempered participant. This chapter focuses on those instances in which the spectator becomes a plaintiff in a civil suit.

Of primary concern here is the spectator's cause of action against the owner of the sports facility in which the event takes place. The owner's duty of care depends on the status of the plaintiff, who is traditionally categorized as either a trespasser, a licensee, or an invitee. Restatement § 329 defines a trespasser as "a person who enters or remains upon land in possession of another without a privilege to do so created by the possessor's consent or otherwise." Restatement § 330 defines a licensee as "a person who is privileged to enter or remain on land only by virtue of the possessor's consent." Restatement § 332 defines an invitee as either a "public invitee" or a "business visitor." A public invitee is "a person who is invited to enter or remain on land as a member of the public for a purpose for which the land is held open to the public." A business visitor is "a person who is invited to enter or remain on land for a purpose directly or indirectly connected with business dealings with the possessor of land."

The trespasser is the least-protected class of plaintiffs. The traditional common law rule was that the possessor owed no duty to trespassers to make the premises safe. The only duty owed was to refrain from intentionally harming the trespasser. Over the years, a number of exceptions have been recognized. Although the precise nature of the duty owed varies from state to state, it is fair to say that a somewhat greater duty is owed when the presence of the trespasser is known or when the trespass is frequent over a limited portion of the land, or when the trespasser is a child endangered by an artificial condition (the so-called attractive nuisance doctrine).

The basic duty owed to a licensee is to warn of known dangers. The duty owed to an invitee is greater, encompassing those dangers which a reasonable inspection would have revealed. Furthermore, as far as an invitee is concerned, a warning is not sufficient if the condition is very dangerous. Thus, there is a duty to repair highly dangerous conditions to protect the invitee.

The ticket-holding spectator would clearly be an invitee to whom the highest duty of care is owed. A question arises as to the status of those who enter the facility without a ticket—for example, a spectator who enters at halftime of a game when the ticket-takers go off duty and the gates are opened. No reported cases address this issue. Rational arguments could be made that such a spectator fits any of the three categories.

Assumption of risk plays a vital role in cases involving injuries to spectators. Through a long line of cases, courts have generally agreed that spectators at sporting events assume the risks commonly associated with observing the sport. Weistart and Lowell, referring to this rule as the common knowledge rule, at 951, state that "spectators at sports activities assume, as a matter of law, all of the ordinary and inherent risks of the sport which they are observing." Thus, the baseball fan struck by a foul ball cannot recover. But the common knowledge rule is not so easy in cases involving less obvious assumptions of risk. The material that follows examines these cases, along with others, in which the defendant is not the owner of the sports facility but, rather, is another spectator or a participant.

THE LANDMARK CASE

[Candor compels an admission that *Schentzel*, which follows, is not so much a landmark case as it is a case representative of the hundreds of reported spectator-versus-owner cases. A good collection of these cases appears in the footnotes accompanying the text of Weistart and Lowell, pp. 951–965.]

Schentzel v. Philadelphia National League Club
173 Pa. Super. 179, 96 A.2d 181 (1953)

[A woman attending a baseball game for the first time was struck by a foul ball and injured. She sued the owners of the club and field on a negligence-based theory and recovered a judgment at the trial court level. The court here reverses.]

"Negligence" is the doing of that which a reasonably prudent man would not do under the circumstances, or the failing to do that which a reasonably prudent man would do under the circumstances. [Citation omitted.]

· · · · · · · ·

Plaintiff contends that the legal duty owing her by defendant (which she claims was breached) consisted of "exceptional precautions" toward its women patrons, many of whom are ignorant of the hazards involved in the game, and who are induced to attend by special invitation, as on afternoons when they are admitted free; that exceptional precautions include extension of the screen coverage behind the batter's and catcher's positions to a wider area, still leaving "a few sections" for patrons who prefer to watch the game from unprotected areas. In substance the argument is tantamount to a request for a holding that a baseball club must at its peril always have available a seat behind the screen whenever a patron requests one. The plaintiff has furnished no proof that the screening of a wider area would have resulted in her being seated within it, thus, by inference, precluding her injury. . . . The Supreme Court of Minnesota was confronted with a similar problem in *Brisson v. Minneapolis Baseball & Athletic Ass'n.*, 185 Minn. 507, 240 N.W. 903, 904 (1932). In holding that the management is under no duty to provide screened seats for all who desire them, regardless of the number of patrons present, the Court stated: "In our opinion they [defendants] exercise the required care if they provide screen for the most dangerous part of the grand stand and for those who may be reasonably anticipated to desire protected seats, and that they need not provide such seats for an unusual crowd, such as the one in attendance at the game here involved." [Citations omitted.]

In this case, plaintiff produced no evidence tending to show that defendant's screening of certain sections of its grandstand deviated from that customarily employed at other baseball parks. The courts of this Commonwealth have adhered to general usage as a test of negligence with respect to methods and appliances employed in business and have held that in the absence of proof *by plaintiff* that defendant deviated from ordinary standards the question of negligence is not for the jury. . . . [Citations omitted.]

No claim is made that the screen was defective in structure. The only question of defectiveness relates to the extent of coverage. It is of record that the screen protected almost all the seats in five sections of defendant's upper stand and practically all of five sections in its lower stand. There is no evidence to indicate the number of seats behind the protective screen. Provided with such meagre background of evidence, the jury were nevertheless permitted to set a theoretical standard of due care upon which to predicate their finding of negligence. We think their verdict under these circumstances cannot represent more than mere conjecture. . . .

Appellant contends that plaintiff has produced no evidence of negligence on its part and argues that as a spectator at its baseball game she voluntarily assumed the risk of being struck by batted or thrown balls. It is clear that plaintiff did not *expressly* consent to accept the hazard which caused her injury. However, consent may be implied from conduct under the circumstances. We quote at length from Prosser on Torts at 383–384: "By entering freely and voluntarily into any relation or situation which presents obvious danger, the plaintiff may be taken to accept it, and to agree that he will look out for himself, and relieve the defendant of responsibility. *Those who* participate or *sit as spectators at sports* and amusements *assume all the obvious risks of being hurt.* . . . [Citations omitted.] 'The timorous may stay at home.' " [Chief Justice Cardozo in *Murphy v. Steeplechase Amusement Co.*, 250 N.Y. 479, 166 N.E. 173]. . . .

Plaintiff argues that the danger, as to her, was not obvious and that she cannot be held to have had full knowledge of the risk because this was her first baseball game. Laying aside any imputation to her of the knowledge and appreciation of the danger possessed by her husband, the answer to her argument appears in this further quotation from Prosser at 387–388: "Since the basis of assumption of risk is not so much knowledge of the risk as the consent to assume it, it is possible for the plaintiff to assume risks of whose specific existence he is not aware. He may, in other words, consent to take his chances as to unknown conditions. . . . In general, the boundaries of an assumption of risk coincide with those of the defendant's obligation of care. They are not, however, invariably identical, since the defendant may be free to proceed upon the supposition that the plaintiff understands the risk and undertakes to protect himself against it, although the plaintiff is in fact ignorant of the risk and does not consent to assume it. The distinction is well illustrated by *Ingersoll v. Onondaga Hockey Club*, 245 App. Div. 137, 281 N.Y.S. 505, in which it was held that the owner of a hockey rink was not required to ask each entering patron whether he had ever witnessed a hockey game before, but might reasonably assume that the danger of being hit by the puck would be understood and accepted."

Plaintiff was a woman 47 years of age. There is nothing whatever in the record to support an inference that she was of inferior intelligence, that she had subnormal perception, or that she had led a cloistered life. Consequently, she must be presumed to have been cognizant of the "neighborhood knowledge" with which individuals living in organized society are normally equipped. We think the frequency with which foul balls go astray, alight in the grandstand or field, and are sometimes caught and retained by onlookers at the baseball games is a matter of such common everyday practical knowledge as to be a subject of judicial notice. It strains our collective imagination to visualize the situation of the wife of a man obviously interested in the game, whose children view the games on the home television set, and who lives in a metropolitan community, so far removed from that knowledge as not to be chargeable with it.

The problem here presented is one of first impression with us. As stated by the learned court below, there is authority in other jurisdictions "the tenor [of which] appears to be that one attending a baseball game assumes a risk of the ordinary dangers inherent in the game, and that persons of ordinary intelligence and experience are presumed to be aware of such dangers," while "there are other decisions clearly indicating that in the absence of knowledge of the dangers involved in watching a baseball game, a patron does not assume the risk of injury by attending a game." The only vaguely close approximation to the present factual situation within this jurisdiction is that of *Douglas v. Converse, supra,* 248 Pa. 232, 93 A. 955. There a spectator at a polo game brought an action for damages against one of the players for injuries incurred when the latter's horse went beyond the boundaries of the field and struck him. In the *Douglas* case the issue was whether defendant was negligent in failing to maintain control over his horse. The Court, in reversing the nonsuit entered by the lower court and in awarding a new trial, held that it was within the province of the jury under all the evidence to decide whether the horse had become unmanageable. At page 235 of 248 Pa., at page 956 of 93 A., the Court set forth the guiding principle, viz.: "*There is in the game of polo the element of risk, and both players and bystanders assumed the chance of the ordinary dangers incident to the game in participating in and witnessing the contest.* Spectators, however, do not assume a risk which results from reckless playing, or the failure of a player to control and guide a horse so as to avoid accident when such control is reasonably possible" (Italics supplied). In that case the injury was caused by an animate agency which was under the immediate and constant control—or at least potentially so—of the defendant player. In the present situation, once the impact with the bat caused the ball to move in an unintended direction, all possible control over it vanished. The Court in the *Douglas* case intimated that the serious accident involved more than "the chance of the ordinary dangers incident to the game" assumed by bystanders.

In *Keys v. Alamo City Baseball Co., supra,* Tex.Civ.App., 150 S.W.2d 368, plaintiff was injured by being struck by a foul ball at defendant's stadium. She had never attended a game before and was ignorant of the risk involved. Judgment n.o.v. was affirmed, the Court holding that there was no reason for defendant to be aware of plaintiff's lack of appreciation of the danger and that it would be "absurd" to require the ticket seller or other employee to warn each patron that he or she would be imperilled by "vagrant baseballs" in unscreened areas of the grandstand.

Anderson v. Kansas City Baseball Club, Mo.Sup., 231 S.W.2d 170, is similar in principle. Plaintiff alleged that she was wholly unaware of the hazards of baseball and that defendant was negligent in seating her in an unscreened portion of its grandstand. She had been seated behind the screen but was requested by an usher to vacate to another seat in the unscreened section, which he assured her was safe. In finding that the complaint did not state a cause of action the Missouri Court held that there was no duty on the part of a proprietor to warn an invitee of activities which do not involve an "unreasonable risk" of harm to him, that the risks and hazards did not result from any negligence on the part of defendant but rather were obvious and inherent in the game itself, and that it did not believe that plaintiff's alleged inquiry as to the safety of an unscreened seat imposed upon defendant a duty to warn which did not otherwise exist.

The plaintiff in *Brown v. San Francisco Ball Club, Inc., supra*, 99 Cal. App. 484, 222 P.2d 19, 21, likewise alleged ignorance of the risk attendant upon viewing a baseball game and that she could not, therefore, have assumed it knowingly. In disposing of this contention the Court made the pertinent observation that plaintiff was "a mature person in possession of her faculties," "46 years of age," who had seen one baseball game prior to the one at which she was injured but "did not see balls thrown or knocked into the crowd," and stated:

We find nothing here to take appellant outside the usual rule, whether it be said that this 'common knowledge' of these obvious and inherent risks are imputed to her or that they are obvious risks which should have been observed by her in the exercise of ordinary care.

In *Blakeley v. White Star Line*, 154 Mich. 635, 118 N.W. 482, 483, 19 L.R.A., N.S., 772, the Michigan Supreme Court stated: "It is knowledge common to all that in these games [of baseball] hard balls are thrown and batted with great swiftness; that they are liable to be muffed or batted or thrown outside the lines of the diamond, and visitors standing in position that may be reached by such balls have voluntarily placed themselves there with knowledge of the situation, and may be held to assume the risk." This early dictum was quoted with approval in *Crane v. Kansas City Baseball & Exhibition Co.*, 168 Mo. App. 301, 153 S.W. 1076.

On a motion for judgment n.o.v. the testimony must be viewed in the light most favorable to the plaintiff and she must be given the benefit of every fact and every reasonable inference of fact arising therefrom, and any conflict in the evidence must be resolved in her favor. *Menzel v. Lamproplos*, 168 Pa.Super. 329, 77 A.2d 645. Despite this benefit, we think that as a matter of law plaintiff has failed to prove negligence on the part of defendant, and that she must be charged with an implied assumption of the normal and ordinary risks incident to attendance at a baseball game.

. . . .

Judgment reversed and here entered for defendant.

AUTHOR'S NOTE—THE SPECTATOR AS PLAINTIFF

Baseball

The general rule respecting baseball is that spectators are presumed to know that at certain times batted balls will be hit into the stands; therefore, they are said to have assumed the risk. One of the earliest reported cases, *Crane v. Kansas City Baseball Exhibition Co.*, 168 Mo. App. 301, 303 153 S.W. 1076, 1077 (1913), noted that "baseball is our national game, and the rules governing it, and the manner in which it is played, and the risks and dangers incident thereto are matters of common knowledge." Courts generally charge spectators with knowledge that, "in baseball games hard balls are thrown and batted with great swiftness, that they are liable to be thrown or batted outside the lines of the diamond, and that spectators in positions which may be reached by such balls assume the risk thereof" (*Cincinnati Baseball Club Co. v. Eno*, 112 Ohio St. 175, 180, 147 N.E. 86, 87 (1925)). In *Brisson v. Minneapolis Baseball & Athletic Ass'n*, 185 Minn. 507, 509, 240 N.W. 903, 904 (1932), the Minnesota Supreme Court stated:

No one of ordinary intelligence could see many innings of the ordinary game without coming to a full realization that batters cannot and do not control the direction of the ball which they strike and that foul tips or liners may go in an entirely unexpected direction. He could not hear the bat strike the ball many times without realizing that the ball was a hard object. Even the sound of the contact of the ball with the gloves would soon apprise him of that.

In many cases involving injured baseball spectators, it is claimed that the defendant is obligated to provide protective screening for all seats rather than for only the few seats located directly behind home plate. The majority of cases appear to hold, however, that the park owner is obligated to furnish just a reasonable number of protected seats and that a spectator assumes the risk by sitting elsewhere. A contention that the entire park should be enclosed by a protective screen was rejected by a Wisconsin court as unreasonable because

The interest, the popularity and the game of baseball as a national pastime would be doomed for the excitement and enthusiasm is so eloquently displayed to the Court's own eyes that the chasing or retrieving of a foul ball in the stands, sometimes to the detriment of others, would be drastically curtailed, and a thing of the past for our American souvenir loving sport spectators. (*Powless v. Milwaukee County*, 6 Wis. 2d 78, 84, 94 N.W.2d 187, 190 (1959).)

If a spectator sits in an unprotected seat, he is deemed to have assumed the risk. Further, as already noted, where a plaintiff was relegated to an unscreened seat even though she requested a protected seat, a subsequent injury was found to be noncompensable (*Brisson v. Minneapolis Baseball & Athletic Ass'n*, 185 Minn. 507, 240 N.W. 903 (1932)).

There is no assumption of risk when a ball passes through the protective screen and injures the spectator. The park owner will be held liable. For example, see *Edling v. Kansas City Baseball & Exhibition Co.*, 181 Mo. App. 327, 168 S.W. 908 (1914). However, if a ball flies over (*Hull v. Oklahoma City Baseball Co.*, 196 Okla. 40, 163 P.2d 982 (1945)) or sails around (*Wells v. Minneapolis Baseball & Athletic Ass'n*, 122 Minn. 327, 142 N.W. 706 (1913)) the protective screening, the owner is generally not liable on the theory of assumption of risk, contributory negligence, or lack of proximate cause. For example, in *Jones v. Alexandria Baseball Ass'n, Inc.*, 50 So.2d 93, 94 (La. Ct. App. 1951) the ball sailed over the screen behind which the plaintiff was sitting. He watched the ball until it went beyond him and turned around to resume watching the game. The ball struck a light pole and shot back into the crowd, hitting and fracturing the plaintiff's jaw. The court denied recovery and stated, "It seems to us that one of the accepted maxims of the game of golf is most appropriate in this instance and that is that plaintiff's injury is attributable to his own fault in failing to 'keep his eye on the ball.' "

Therefore, there is little question today that the baseball fan assumes the risk of injury from hazards incident to the game, such as foul balls, line drives, and wild throws. In *Shaw v. Boston American League Baseball Co.*, 325 Mass. 419, 422, 90 N.E.2d 840, 842 (1950), the Massachusetts Supreme Judicial Court held that the owner of a baseball park owes no duty to warn the spectator of foul balls falling in the unscreened areas of the stands. In an action based on an injury suffered from an errant baseball, no jury question is presented; there is no duty to warn of the obvious dangers, and as a matter of law, "a spectator familiar with the game assumes reasonable risks and hazards inherent in the game."

Ice Hockey

Hockey is a relative newcomer on the American sporting scene. In a short time, hockey's inherent dangers have caused a great deal of litigation. The question of owners' liability is not as well settled as in baseball. Many jurisdictions that have dealt with this issue state that hockey, unlike baseball, is a new sport; therefore, inexperienced spectators cannot be held chargeable with knowledge of the game's dangers, and they do not assume the risk as a matter of law.

Thus, while a spectator may not recover for a baseball injury, he may recover for an injury caused by a flying puck. *Morris v. Cleveland Hockey Club, Inc.*, 157 Ohio St. 225, 237, 105 N.E.2d 419, 426 (1952), states the majority's rationale: "There is sound reasoning for the baseball rule. Baseball is the national pastime of the U.S. . . . Although hockey is becoming ever more popular, it is not nearly so universally played as is baseball and, as we have pointed out, its dangers are certainly not so obvious to a stranger to the game as would be dangers incident to baseball."

A number of courts, including California, (*Shurman v. Fresno Ice Rink, Inc.*, 91 Cal. App. 2d 469, 205 P.2d 77 (1949)), Massachusetts, (*Shanney v. Boston Madison Square Garden Corp.*, 296 Mass. 168, 5 N.E.2d 1 (1936)), Nebraska, (*Tite v. Omaha Coliseum Corp.*, 144 Neb. 22, 12 N.W.2d 90 (1943)), and Rhode Island, (*James v. Rhode Island Auditorium, Inc.*, 60 R.I. 405, 199 A. 293 (1938)), have adopted the "no assumption of risk" rule. In *Lemoine v. Springfield Hockey Association*, 307 Mass. 102, 29 N.E.2d 716 (1940), for example, the plaintiff, who had been attending games for three to four years, was struck by a puck while walking toward the restroom. The question of his assumption of risk was regarded as a jury question, and the plaintiff recovered. In *James v. Rhode Island Auditorium, Inc.*, a spectator was struck by a puck while seated in an unscreened area of the arena. Although the plaintiff was found to have had no personal awareness of the dangers involved, the defendant argued that no distinction should be drawn between the baseball and the hockey spectator. The court rejected this argument stating that the risks incidental to attendance at a hockey game were not as well known as those involved in attending a baseball game. The plaintiff was justified in believing that the seat he occupied was reasonably safe, and he did not, as a matter of law, assume the risk of his injury.

The following jurisdictions have held that baseball and hockey are indistinguishable: Minnesota, (*Modec v. City of Eveleth*, 224 Minn. 556, 29 N.W.2d 453 (1947)), Michigan, (*Wolf v. Olympia Stadium, Inc.*, Nos. 247–609, 247–610 (Wayne County Cir.Ct., Mich., 1949)), and New York, (*Kaufman v. Madison Square Garden Corp.*, 246 A.D. 589, 284 N.Y.S. 808 (1935)). Therefore, the spectator assumes the risk. *Hammel v. Madison*

Square Garden Corp., 156 Misc. 311, 312, 279 N.Y.S. 815, 816 (1935), established this position: "There are, however, a number of cases where spectators at baseball games have been injured by batted balls coming into the stands. The consensus of opinion in those cases is that there is no liability; that spectators occupying seats that are not screened assume the risk incident thereto. The baseball cases seem to present the same legal question that confronts us here."

Minnesota, New York, and Michigan are clearly among the areas where the sport of hockey has been established the longest. It is not surprising that hockey is treated in the same manner as baseball. Hockey is a relatively new sport in many of the jurisdictions that do allow recovery. Thus, the essential problem may be in determining how prevalent hockey is in each jurisdiction. There is a great likelihood that when, in a particular jurisdiction, hockey is as much a matter of common knowledge as is baseball, the courts will implement the general rule that the spectator assumes the risk of injury when attending a hockey game.

Because the cases that distinguish baseball and hockey are not recent, there may be some doubt as to their continued validity in light of the dramatic expansion of professional hockey.

Auto Racing

There is little doubt that the extreme danger involved in auto racing has been an important factor in making auto racing popular. The spectators, of course, do not expect to share in this danger. The majority of American jurisdictions hold that the promoters of an auto race must provide adequate barriers for the protection of spectators. In *Saari v. State*, 203 Misc. 859, 866, 119 N.Y.S.2d 507, 516 (1953), the court said: Because risk to spectators and participants from automobile races is high, "the standard of care must likewise be high. One who conducts or sponsors such an event is . . . negligent unless he uses a high degree of care to provide adequate safeguards against reasonably foreseeable dangers to spectators and enforces the observation of such safeguards and precautions both by participants and spectators."

Are the dangers of auto racing obvious enough to the spectator? It appears that the majority of courts hold that injured spectators do not assume the risk. A landmark case in this area is *Arnold v. State*, 163 A.D. 253, 148 N.Y.S. 479 (1914) in which a racer crashed through a wooden fence killing eleven spectators and injuring several more. The court held that the State of New York, the race's sponsor, had breached its positive duty to guard against the possibility of a car leaving the track and had to compensate the victims for their injuries. Assumption of risk was not an effective defense.

The Supreme Judicial Court of Massachusetts confirmed this position in *Alden v. Norwood Arena, Inc.*, 332 Mass. 267, 124 N.E.2d 505 (1955).

This was an action against a stock-car race operator for death and injuries suffered by spectators when a wheel from a racer flew into the grandstand. The court held that the promoter owed the spectators a duty of due care to see that the premises were reasonably safe for their intended use and to warn them of dangers which were not so obvious. The risk of being hit by a flying automobile wheel as an incident inherent in the sport of automobile racing was not obvious to the spectator of ordinary intelligence; therefore, spectators who were injured while attending the stock-car race did not assume, as a matter of law, the risk of such injury.

A minority of jurisdictions have concluded that if the race track has made some provision for the safety of spectators, the spectator will be charged with assumption of risk. In *Blake v. Fried*, 173 Pa. Super 27, 95 A.2d 360 (1953), the operators of a stock-car race track encircled the track with a heavy guard rail three feet high and installed reinforced wire-mesh fence fourteen feet high around the track. The court held that because the defendant's conduct was reasonable in light of what they could anticipate, they were not negligent. Therefore, they were not liable for the injuries sustained by grandstand spectators when a wheel came off a stock car, hit a guard rail, and bounced over the fence into the grandstand.

Horse Racing

A number of jurisdictions hold that spectators at a horse race assume the risk of injury if the horse jumps over the rail. In *Gulf Stream Park Racing Association v. Miller*, 119 So.2d 749 (Fla. Dist. Ct. App. 1960), a horse threw its rider and raced around the track several times before jumping into the crowd and injuring a spectator. Although the defendant made no attempt to corral the horse, the court found no negligence, as a matter of law, and reversed the verdict for the plaintiff. Because of the improved construction of race tracks, the horse race accident has largely become a thing of the past. There has been virtually no litigation in this area in the past 40 years.

Golf

The game of golf has stirred up an enormous amount of litigation, second only to baseball. Golf litigation arises under three basic sets of circumstances. The first involves the golfer who hits the ball in the intended direction. He is held to two duties: he must make sure no one is within the area toward which he is aiming, and he must give an audible warning prior to hitting the ball. Warning given after the ball is hit is insufficient (*Biskup v. Hoffman*, 220 Mo. App. 542, 287 S.W. 865 (1926)). The second situation occurs when the defendant's shot "hooks" or "slices" in a completely unanticipated direction and strikes someone on the golf course. When this happens the defendant is not liable and the injured plaintiff is held to have assumed the risk (*Houston* v. *Escott*, 85 F. Supp. (D. Del. 1949)). Finally, if a golf ball injures a person who is not on the golf course, as for example on an adjoining roadway, the defendant has generally been held to be liable. (*Westborough Country Club* v. *Palmer*, 204 F.2d 143 (8th Cir. 1953); *Townsley v. State*, 6 Misc. 2d 557, 164 N.Y.S.2d 840 (1957)).

Wrestling

The sport of wrestling has created a surprising amount of litigation. A spectator sued a promoter for injuries sustained when a wrestler was thrown from the ring onto the spectator's lap in *Dusckiewicz v. Carter*, 115 Vt. 122, 52 A.2d 788 (1947). The Vermont court, in holding that the defendant's motion for a directed verdict should not have been granted, said, "An invitee at a place of amusement ordinarily assumes the risk of an obvious danger or one that is of common knowledge; conversely, such a person does not assume the risk of a hidden or undisclosed danger, not of common knowledge, in the absence of warning or personal knowledge" (*Id.* at 125, 52 A.2d at 791). Thus, the court followed the majority rule by holding that this type of risk is one which a spectator does not assume.

Injuries Caused by Unsafe Premises—No Assumption of Risk

Owners and operators of sporting arenas have the duty to maintain the premises in a reasonably safe condition and to supervise the conduct of spectators on the premises to prevent injury. Therefore, a spectator attending an athletic event may assume that the owner or operator has exercised reasonable care to make the facilities safe for the purposes of the invitation.

In *Edling v. Kansas City Baseball & Exhibition Co.*, 181 Mo. App. 327, 329, 168 S.W. 908, 909 (1914), the plaintiff was injured when a foul ball passed through a large hole in the netting behind which he was sitting, struck him in the face, and broke his nose. The plaintiff's petition alleged:

That the defendants negligently and carelessly permitted the screening on said grandstand to be and become old, rotten, worn, and defective, and negligently and carelessly permitted holes large enough to permit the passage of a baseball to be and remain in said screening in said grandstand; and that defendants knew of said old, worn, rotten, and dangerous condition of said screening, or, by the exercise of ordinary care, could have known of same long prior to the accident to plaintiff hereinafter complained of, and in time, by the exercise of ordinary care, to have repaired the same prior to said accident.

The court found that an owner who maintains a baseball park for profit must exercise reasonable care to protect its patrons against injuries by foul balls. If the owner screens a part of the grandstand exposed to foul balls, it is implied that he assures patrons paying for admission thereto that seats behind the screen are reasonably protected, and he must exercise reasonable care to keep the screens free from defects or be guilty of negligence.

In *Rockwell v. Hillcrest Country Club, Inc.*, 25 Mich. App. 276, 181 N.W.2d 290 (1970), a suspension bridge crossing a river on a golf course collapsed; its occupants dropped into the river below. At the time of the collapse, there were approximately 80 to 100 golf spectators on the bridge, along with a golf cart. All the spectators were watching a tournament being played on the course. Among the spectators were plaintiffs James and Ann Rockwell. Ann Rockwell fell 25 feet, struck the water, broke her back, and sustained permanent injuries.

The evidence produced at trial showed that the bridge was constructed to hold 25 people safely; when it collapsed, there were 80 to 100 people on the bridge; no sign was present warning those using the bridge of its safe capacity and no supervisory personnel were present to oversee proper use of the bridge. In affirming a judgment for the plaintiffs the court stated:

The obligation of reasonable care is a full one, applicable in all respects, and extending to everything that threatens the invitee with an unreasonable risk of harm. The occupier must not only use care not to injure the visitor by negligent acts, and to warn him of latent dangers of which the occupier knows, but he must also take reasonable precautions to protect the invitee from dangers which are foreseeable from the arrangement or use. The obligation extends to the original construction of the premises, where it results in a dangerous condition. (*Id.* at 281–282, N.W. 2d at 293)

In *Johnson v. Zemel*, 109 N.J.L. 197, 160 A. 356 (1932), the plaintiff was injured when he stepped into a hole in an aisle while attending a boxing match. The court found that where the owner of a hall lets it out for public purposes, he thereby holds out to the public that it is safe, and he is bound to use reasonable care to see that it has been properly constructed and is maintained in fit condition for the purposes for which it is used. Thus, the owner is responsible for injuries sustained by spectators which result from his failure to maintain the premises in a safe condition.

Although it deals with liability to a participant rather than a spectator, *Dawson v. Rhode Island Auditorium*, 104 R.I. 116, 242 A.2d 407 (1968), is instructive. In *Dawson*, a member of the Harlem Magicians basketball team slipped on a puddle of water on the basketball court while driving toward the basket. The wet spot was the result of a leak in the roof. In allowing recovery the court noted:

in order for defendant to exculpate [itself] . . . [it] had to show . . . [once] having become aware of the leaky roof, it had undertaken such actions which would assure a reasonable auditorium owner that all the leaks in its building were corrected . . . or secondly, to show, as an alternative . . . it had apprised plaintiff, before his scheduled performance on the court, of the actual conditions of the building and at the same time issued him a warning of the risk of harm which those conditions presented to anyone choosing to play basketball at defendant's auditorium (*Id.* at 129, 242 A.2d at 415).

The Spectator versus the Participant and the Participant's Employer

A wholly separate category of cases involves situations in which the spectator is injured by the arguably tortious conduct of a participant. In *Payne v. Maple Leaf Gardens Ltd.*, [1949] 1 D.L.R. 369 (Ont. Ca.), a season ticketholder was struck by the stick of a hockey player who was engaged in a fight with another player. The plaintiff recovered from the player. The court noted that this was not a risk assumed by the spectator. The plaintiff was unable, however, to impose liability vicariously on the team because the court found that fighting was outside the scope of employment—a highly questionable finding for anyone familiar with hockey.

Bonetti v. Double Play Tavern, 126 Cal. App. 2d 848, 274 P.2d 751 (1954), involved an action against the sponsor of a baseball team for personal injuries sustained by the plaintiff. Plaintiff was struck by a baseball thrown out of the park by a team member in a fit of anger. Evidence at the trial established that the operators of Double Play Tavern sponsored a semi-pro baseball team, appropriately named "Double Play." On the night of October 27, 1949, the "Double Play" team and the "Bartenders" were engaged in the season finale for the league championship. In the bottom of the ninth inning, with "Double Play" in the field, the score tied at zero, and the bases loaded, Paul Hjort, the "Double Play" left fielder dropped a high pop fly, and the winning run scored. In anger, Hjort picked up the ball and threw it out of the park in the direction of the Standard Oil Service Station located on the corner. The plaintiff, who was walking across the station property to get into her fiancé's car, was struck on the side of her head and knocked to the ground.

The court held that the defendant tavern operators were liable because "in practically all jurisdictions, the law is now settled that a master is liable for the willful and malicious acts of his servant when done within the scope of his employment" (*Id.* at 852, 274 P. 2d at 754). In reasoning that Hjort's acts were within the scope of his employment, the court said:

Where the injury is suffered from a baseball thrown immediately after the player had dropped it, with the consequent loss of the game and championship, at a time when all the players were at a competitively high nervous pitch, in a sport where "hustle" and "fight" are fostered and encouraged, it is not too difficult to conclude that a player might well, in frustration, take the ball and heave it out of the lot, and that such conduct might well be expected by the master. The breaking of clubs, bats and sticks by excited players is a matter of common knowledge to all sportswise persons (*Id.* at 852, 274 P. 2d at 754).

In a vigorous dissent, Judge Molkenbuhr relied on Section 2338 of the California Civil Code, which reads in part: "A principal is responsible to third persons for . . . wrongful acts committed by such agent *in and as a part of the transaction of business*" (*Id.* at 853, 274 P. 2d at 755). Judge Molkenbuhr's opinion was that the act of the left fielder in deliberately throwing the ball out of the park was not an act "in and as a part of the principal's business—that of playing baseball" (*Id.* at 854, 274 P. 2d at 755). Though the principal is required to anticipate any reasonably probable happening, the tort herein complained of was one which under ordinary circumstances could not have been anticipated. Consequently, the defendant tavern operator should not be held liable.

Bonetti can be contrasted with *Atlanta Baseball Co. v. Lawrence*, 38 Ga. App. 497, 144 S.E. 351 (1928), in which a baseball player employed by the proprietor of a baseball park left his position in the field, entered the grandstand, and assaulted a spectator who had criticized his play. The court held that the assault was not committed within the scope of his employment nor in the pursuit of his master's business. The court reasoned that "if the defendant had had good reason to apprehend that such a thing would probably happen, then it should have exercised reasonable care to prevent the occurrence, but it was not required to anticipate the improbable, nor to take measures to prevent a happening which no reasonable person would have expected" (*Id.* at 500, 144 S.E. at 353). In *Wiersma v. City of Long Beach*, 41 Cal. App. 2d 8, 106 P.2d 45 (1940), a wrestler jumped out of the ring and attacked the plaintiff with a chair. The defendant wrestler was deemed to be acting outside the scope of his employment, and the defendant promoter was exonerated.

The cases have their own curious logic. For purposes of imposing vicarious liability, courts are guided by some notion of foreseeable participant behavior. While Hjort's post-game tantrum was foreseeable, the gratuitous violence in *Atlanta Baseball* and *Wiersma* arguably was not. Presumably, vicarious liability could be imposed even in cases like *Payne* if the employer knew of the employee's propensity for such behavior. Otherwise, such attacks likely will be viewed as outside the scope of employment. (See, for example, *Tomjanovich*, discussed in Chapter 1.)

Summary

As a general rule, a spectator will be deemed to have assumed only the ordinary and inherent risks of attending a sporting event. In regard to unsafe premises at a sports facility, the owner or operator of such facility is bound to use reasonable care to see that it has been properly constructed and is maintained in fit condition for the purposes for which it is used. Thus, the owner or operator of a sporting facility has a duty to maintain the premises in a reasonably safe condition and will be liable for a breach of this duty in the absence of contributory negligence. In the realm of master-servant liability, whether an injury to a spectator is compensable turns on whether the employer should have reasonably anticipated the injurious act by the employee. If a court finds that the act committed by the employee was a probable occurrence, which the employer should have reasonably anticipated, then the employer will be held liable.

THE NOT-SO-HYPOTHETICAL CASE OF THE FAN IN THE FRONT ROW VERSUS JOHN MCENROE

Sports fans no doubt have their own favorite anecdotal accounts of occurrences in which players "go after" spectators. Among Jimmy Piersall's many memorable antics were confrontations with heckling fans. A few years ago, Cesar Cedeno ventured into the stands after a heckler who crossed the line by jabbering about an incident that has haunted Cedeno—an incident in which a young girl was found dead in Cedeno's motel room. But it is perhaps John McEnroe, more than any single performer, who is best suited to be considered as our hypothetical defendant.

McEnroe, it can fairly be said, has a marked propensity for losing his cool while playing tennis. While no one can doubt that he is a tennis-playing genius, many quarrel with his on-the-court antics—replete with thrown rackets, batted balls, and epithets galore. At the United States Open in 1983, McEnroe had a temper tantrum he may regret. In an incident captured by the television cameras, McEnroe threw sawdust in the face of a front-row fan who was, in McEnroe's opinion, too forthright and vociferous in rooting for McEnroe's opponent. This incident has given rise to litigation which is pending as of this writing. This note explores the issues arising out of this occurrence.

The Fan's Causes of Action

Even if we assume that our hypothetical fan did not suffer physical harm as a result of the McEnroe attack, three causes of action are clearly viable—offensive battery, assault, and intentional or reckless infliction of severe emotional distress by extreme and outrageous conduct. And it would further appear that McEnroe is defenseless. In short, the legal issues are rather straightforward and uncomplicated. The success of the law suit will turn on a policy matter, which will be examined after a brief consideration of the causes of action.

The offensive battery cause of action is virtually unassailable. It is difficult to see how liability can be avoided. McEnroe had the requisite intent and caused a contact which is clearly offensive. Restatement § 19 says "a bodily contact is offensive if it offends a reasonable sense of personal dignity." Comment a. elaborates: "In order that a contact be offensive to a reasonable sense of personal dignity, it must be one which would offend the ordinary person and as such one not unduly sensitive as to his personal dignity. It must, therefore, be a contact which is unwarranted by the social usages prevalent at the time and place at which it is inflicted."

If the plaintiff was placed in apprehension of the battery (that is, if the plaintiff "saw it coming"), an assault cause of action would also be available. Again, physical harm is not an element of the cause of action. Assault is designed to protect the mental interest in being free from apprehension of battery.

Finally, our fan would appear also to have a good cause of action for intentional or reckless infliction of severe emotional distress. Restatement § 46 defines this tort as follows: "(1) One who by extreme and outrageous conduct intentionally or recklessly causes severe emotional distress to another is subject to liability for such emotional distress." Comment d. explains: "Liability has been found only where the conduct has been so outrageous in character, and so extreme in degree, as to go beyond all possible bounds of decency, and to be regarded as atrocious, and utterly intolerable in a civilized community. Generally, the case is one in which the recitation of the facts to an average member of the community would arouse his resentment against the actor and lead him to exclaim, 'Outrageous!' " With the possible caveat that the average member of the community might be moved to exclaim something more pejorative than "outrageous," McEnroe would appear liable here as well, assuming our plaintiff has indeed suffered "severe" emotional distress.

What defenses are available to McEnroe? Even if our fan did provoke McEnroe by rooting for the opponent, the short answer is that Mc-

Enroe has no real viable defense. In short, no recognized privilege could be claimed by McEnroe. (See Chapter 1 for discussion of privilege.)

Moreover, it should be pointed out that punitive damages are generally available in each of the aforementioned causes of action. This means that the plaintiff may properly inquire about the defendant's personal wealth—a prospect most appealing to the plaintiff in this case—in order to assist the fact-finder in arriving at a fair punitive award. An award equivalent to what McEnroe would make in one month would no doubt be a healthy sum.

The Policy Issue

The basic policy issue presented here is timeworn. As a matter of policy, do we regard such affronts as legally sufficient grievances? Professor Magruder, in his landmark article, "Mental and Emotional Disturbance in the Law of Torts," 49 HARVARD LAW REVIEW 1033, 1035 (1936) thought not: "Against a large part of the frictions and irritations and clashing of temperaments incident to participation in a community life, a certain toughening of the mental hide is a better protection than the law could ever be." Magruder might well have advised our front-row fan to just "toughen up."

The more modern view, and the one to which a majority of courts now subscribe, would likely permit our fan to get to the jury. Our fan has, after all, suffered a dignitary wrong. Contemporary society is increasingly aware that mental injuries are genuine and compensable. This is simply not the kind of case for which a toughening of the mental hide is the only remedy.

Finally, what better way to deter McEnroe, and others like him, from continuing his anti-social conduct? It would ironically be fitting for a jury to saddle the likes of McEnroe with a huge judgment in a case like this one. Look for a similar result sometime soon.

ADDITIONAL NOTES

1. *Waivers and releases from liability.* In many cases, the sponsors of sporting events draft waivers or releases by which they attempt to avoid liability. These exculpatory agreements are contractual and generally provide that the sponsor is not responsible for harm caused by negligence. The problem that arises in regard to these agreements is that it brings two strong public policies into conflict. One policy highly values freedom of contract. The other deems it important that individuals be answerable for the consequences of their negligence. As might be expected, cases can be found on both sides. For a collection of these cases, see Weistart and Lowell at 969. It should also be noted that waivers

and releases are often used to insulate the owner from liability to participants as well as to spectators. Here, too, the results are mixed. These cases are collected in Weistart and Lowell at 965–968.

2. *The spectator who is denied admission.* A related issue involves the rights of a spectator denied admission to a sporting event. The traditional common law rule gave the owner a broad power to exclude any person for any reason. The leading case is *Morrone v. Washington Jockey Club of the District of Columbia*, 227 U.S. 633 (1913), holding that a ticket does not create a property right and is not a conveyance of an interest in the race track. (The plaintiff was denied admission because of an alleged conspiracy to drug a horse.) The modern trend is to restrict this power, so that patrons are not arbitrarily excluded. Moreover, if the acts of the owner can be fairly regarded as "state-action" for constitutional purposes, the power to exclude is further constrained by the constitutional rights of the spectators. The issue is addressed in detail in Weistart and Lowell at 141–147, 190–195, and 963–965.

3. *Bolton v. Stone*, [1951] A.C. 850, [1951] 1 All E.R. 1078, the classic English sports tort case, cannot pass unnoticed. In *Bolton*, the plaintiff, while walking past a cricket ground maintained by the defendant, was struck by an "altogether exceptional" hit (the cricket equivalent to a "tape measure job"). The House of Lords decided in favor of the defendant and pointed out that although the defendant knew that such a hit was a possibility, the risk of someone being struck by such a hit was so small that the defendant was not obligated to guard against it.

4. *Stampedes and the duty to control crowds.* It is surprising that more injuries are not incurred when crowds get out of control. Not too long ago, a human stampede resulted in the loss of life at a "WHO" concert in Cincinnati. Americans are used to reading about such tragedies at foreign soccer games. Our own national championship games, particularly if the home team wins, raise the spectre of similar tragedies. When the Celtics won the 1984 NBA Championship Series at the Boston Garden, the ensuing melee was frightening. Mobs of spectators tearing down goalposts is a similarly potentially dangerous practice. It is simply a matter of time before Americans are beset by a stampede of epic proportions. What is the duty of the promoter to control the crowd under these circumstances?

5. In *Fish v. Los Angeles Dodgers Baseball Club*, 56 Cal. App. 3d 620, 128 Cal. Rptr 807 (1976), parents of a 14-year-old who died after being hit by a foul ball while attending a Dodgers game sued the Dodgers and a physician. The complaint asserted two theories: (1) failure to provide the boy "with a safe place to witness the ball game" and (2) negligent provision of emergency medical services. The first cause of action was dismissed by the trial court, and the dismissal was affirmed on appeal. The case was submitted to the jury solely on the second is-

sue, which decided in favor of the defendant. On appeal, the court reversed and remanded, holding that the trial court's instructions were erroneous. The court's discussion of intervening causes in medical malpractice cases is especially noteworthy.

The point to be made is that the failure to provide adequate emergency medical assistance to an injured spectator would seem to provide a viable cause of action to the injured spectator, at least to the extent it can be shown that the injuries were aggravated by the lack of such care.

6. *The spectator as a defendant.* There are a number of obvious contexts in which spectators could find themselves on the receiving end of a summons and complaint. Overzealous fans are potential tortfeasors in a variety of fairly common situations, such as throwing debris on the playing surface or at the participants, including referees; fighting for souvenirs; and brawling with opposing fans. A number of years ago, it was quite popular at college football games for a group of fans to engage in what can be described as a "fan toss," wherein a fan was literally tossed about the crowd. If the human plaything is injured, are these fun-loving fans joint tortfeasors?

BIBLIOGRAPHY

Colapietro, Bruno, "The Promoters Liability for Sports Spectator Injuries," 46 CORNELL LAW QUARTERLY 140 (1960).

Conrad, Alfred F., "The Privilege of Forcibly Ejecting an Amusement Patron," 90 UNIVERSITY OF PENNSYLVANIA LAW REVIEW 809 (1942).

"Duty of Baseball Club to Spectator," 24 MICHIGAN LAW REVIEW 76 (1925).

"Injuries to Spectators in the Course of Sporting Activities," 25 MODERN LAW REVIEW 738 (1962).

"Liability of Proprietor of a Baseball Park for Injuries to Spectators Struck by Batted or Thrown Balls," 1951 WASHINGTON UNIVERSITY LAW QUARTERLY 434.

"Owner Liability for Intentional Torts by Professional Athletes Against Spectators," 30 BUFFALO LAW REVIEW (1981).

Pooler, S., "A Survey of the Law on Injuries to Spectators," 39 BOSTON UNIVERSITY LAW REVIEW 54 (1959).

Siskind, Gary E., "Liability for Injuries to Spectators," 6 OSGOOD HALL LAW JOURNAL 305 (1968).

"Theaters and Shows—Assumption of Risk—Spectators at a Baseball Game," 17 MICHIGAN LAW REVIEW 594 (1919).

Thomas, Starr, "Liability of Exhibitors to Spectators at Public Exhibitions: Assumption of Risk," 24 CALIFORNIA LAW REVIEW 429 (1936).

Turner, Max, W. & Kennedy, Frank R., "Exclusion, Ejection, and Segregation of Theater Patrons," 32 IOWA LAW REVIEW 625 (1947).

3

Medical Malpractice in Athletics

It seems obvious that the well-developed, negligence-based principles of medical malpractice apply to sports medicine. As a general rule, the reasonableness of the medical care provided is measured against the minimum common skill of members in good standing of the profession. The "locality rule," which required a doctor to act only up to the standard of the locale in which he or she practiced, is largely a dead letter. The modern trend is to consider the locality of the practice as simply one factor to take into account in assessing the doctor's conduct. Additionally, doctors holding themselves out as specialists are held to a national standard. The issue of "informed consent" looms large. Although "informed consent" is technically an intentional tort defense, modern courts have translated the "informed consent" concept into negligence terminology. Cases thus turn on whether reasonable doctors would have disclosed certain risks. Much of the material that follows illustrates how these basic principles of medical malpractice apply in sports.

Also note, however, that a number of problems are peculiar to sports medicine. One perplexing problem arises out of the somewhat unusual relationships created by the common practice of employing a team doctor. The very term "team doctor" signals the problem. The team doctor owes sometimes conflicting duties to individual team members and the team. The problem manifests itself in situations in which a valuable player is injured before an important game, and the responsibility falls on the team physician to decide if the player can participate. This power to determine eligibility generates a host of other problems. How, for example, is liability to be determined when a doctor permits an injured player to participate and the injury is further aggravated or, worse yet, the athlete dies? Or suppose the doctor refuses to permit the athlete to participate; may the athlete claim a legal right to participate in the face of the medical prohibition?

A number of other problems are especially relevant to athletics. One concerns the extent to which a doctor may properly aid an injured player who wants to participate. To what extent should painkillers and the like be administered to willing athletes? And are the athletes really "willing" under the circumstances? Another problem concerns the use of chemicals to enhance performance. What is the doctor's proper role in this regard? This chapter explores these issues as well.

THE LANDMARK CASES

Welch v. Dunsmuir Joint Union High School District
326 P.2d 633 (Cal. Dist. Ct. App. 1958)

[Anthony Welch, a high school quarterback, was injured on a "quarterback sneak" during a scrimmage. After the play, he was not able to get to his feet. The evidence adduced at trial indicated that when his coach arrived at the scene on the field, Welch was able to move his hands. The team doctor was in attendance, but conflicting evidence was introduced as to whether he examined Welch on or off the field. In any event, eight boys carried Welch off the field. After having been moved from the field, Welch was unable to move his hands. Welch's expert gave the opinion that Welch sustained additional damage to the spinal cord as a consequence of being moved. The jury returned a verdict establishing negligence of both the coach and the doctor. Judgment was entered accordingly, and the court here affirms.]

It appears that after the plaintiff was moved off the field to the sidelines he was unable to move his hands, fingers and feet. With these circumstances in mind the doctor [plaintiff's expert] testified it was his opinion that the plaintiff must have sustained additional damage to the spinal cord after being tackled. The doctor's testimony stands undisputed in the record.

· · · · · · · ·

Defendant contends . . . that the court erred prejudicially in giving an instruction . . . as follows: "Because of the great danger involved in moving an injured human being a person of ordinary prudence will exercise extreme caution when engaged in such an activity. Hence it is the duty of anyone managing or participating in such an activity to exercise extreme caution." Defendant claims that the giving of this instruction was prejudicial for the reason that it set up a false standard of conduct and placed upon the defendant a burden that is not consistent with the existing law. We do not agree with defendant. In this case it appears that the challenged instruction, read with the other instructions, correctly informed the jury that the standard of care required of the defendant was that of ordinary care under the circumstances. [Citations omitted.] Immediately preceding this instruction the court gave the following instruction:

"Inasmuch as the amount of caution used by the ordinarily prudent person varies in direct proportion to the danger known to be involved in his undertaking, it follows that in the exercise of ordinary care, the amount of caution required will vary in accordance with the nature of the act and the surrounding circumstances."

"To put the matter in another way, the amount of caution involved in the exercise of ordinary care, and hence required by law, increases or decreases as does the danger that reasonably should be apprehended." [Citations omitted.]

The standard was still one of ordinary care, that is, of a person of ordinary prudence, where the factual situation shows that great danger was involved in the activity. There was evidence in the case that the moving of a person with suspected grave injuries is inherently a hazardous activity.

· · · · · · · ·

Under the evidence in this case the jury could reasonably have inferred that both the doctor and the coach were negligent in the removal of the plaintiff from the field to the sidelines; the coach in failing to wait for the doctor and allowing plaintiff to be moved, and the doctor in failing to act promptly after plaintiff's injury.

· · · · · · · ·

The judgment is affirmed.

Rosensweig v. State
5 A.D.2d 293, 171 N.Y.S.2d 912 (1958) *aff'd,* **5 N.Y.2d 404, 158 N.E.2d 229 (1959)**

[By statute in New York, all boxers must be examined by a physician. The physician files a report with the State Athletic Commission, which in turn must certify that the fighter is fit before the fighter will be permitted to box.

On August 29, 1951, George Flores was knocked out in the eighth round of a fight at Madison Square Garden. He died four days later from cerebral hemorrhage and edema. Flores had fought on July 24 and

August 14 of 1951, and in both those bouts, he lost by a technical knockout (T.K.O.). Before the August 29 bout, Flores was examined by a physician who certified his fitness to the Commission.

Flores' estate sued the State of New York, alleging that the negligence of the examining physician in certifying Flores' fitness could properly be imputed to the State of New York. At the trial court level, Flores' estate prevailed. The intermediate appellate court reversed, and it is this decision that is excerpted here, because it is one of the few reported cases dealing directly with the liability of a doctor who certifies an athlete as fit. It should be noted that New York's highest court affirmed the intermediate court, but without any discussion of the doctor's negligence. That court limited its discussion to whether the State was vicariously liable for the acts of the doctor, and concluded that, under the circumstances, it was not.]

· · · · · · · ·

Under these circumstances there is serious doubt as to whether the examining doctor is an employee of the State, but, even assuming employment by the State, claimant has not established negligence on the part of the examining doctors.

· · · · · · · ·

The doctor who examined decedent prior to the fatal fight had the benefit of the opinions of doctors who examined decedent after the two previous fights and who found no evidence of brain injury. A signed history given by decedent indicated no symptom of concussion or brain injury. A standard examination revealed no such symptom.

It is urged that there is evidence that some doctors believe it to be better medical practice to withhold permission to engage in another bout to a fighter who has received a severe beating about the head without a lay-off of from two to six months thereafter. It would, of course, be still safer to withhold permission forever. However, there was no official rule requiring such a compulsory lay-off. . . .

For another reason the judgment may not be sustained. It is clear that the immediate proximate cause of the injury which resulted in death was the severe blow to the head which decedent suffered in the final fight. Claimant has failed to establish that this blow alone, irrespective of previous condition, would not have produced the fatal result. [Citations omitted.]

Decedent was engaged in a concededly dangerous activity. From his experience he knew that he would likely be struck by blows to the head. In fact, the very objective of the contestants, well known in advance, is to "knock out" the opponent and cause him to fall to the floor in such condition that he is unable to rise to his feet for a specified time. Decedent assumed the risks known to be inherent in the fight.

· · · · · · · ·

Judgment reversed and claim dismissed, without costs.

Note on *Rosensweig*. Weistart and Lowell are properly critical of the *Rosensweig* reasoning, at 994:

The appellate court obviously disagreed with the trial court's conclusion that there was negligence, but the doctrinal basis for disagreement is not clear. The court stated that a "standard examination" had revealed no injury but gave no indication of what such a standard examination required or what facts indicated that such an examination had been given in the present case. It also noted that the boxer had signed a medical history that disclosed no brain injury, but surely this fact could have little relevance to the negligence of the doctors. . . . In short, the appellate court found no negligence but undertook almost no effort to indicate why it came to that conclusion. Its reasoning would appear to be that a doctor is required to give only a standard examination (which it did not define) and since such examinations had been given here (though it did not say why) there was no basis for a conclusion that the doctors had been negligent.

It should also be noted that the court's glib conclusion that the proximate cause of death was the blow to the head does not preclude a finding that the doctor's negligence in certifying Flores' fitness was also a proximate cause of death.

Colombo v. Sewannaka Central High School District No. 2
87 Misc. 2d 48, 383 N.Y.S.2d 518 (1976)

[John Colombo, a 15-year-old student, was barred from interscholastic participation in contact sports because of a hearing disability. Joined by his parents, he sought to overturn the ban on the ground that it was "arbitrary, capricious, and contrary to law." The court here held that the determination of the school district to follow the advice of its medical director was correct.]

· · · · · · · ·

On December 11, 1975, Dr. Nathan Samuels, the duly designated medical officer for the school district, conducted a physical examination of the petitioner, John, Jr., to determine whether he should be permitted to participate in contact sports in the High School. . . .

The physical examination disclosed no abnormality other than a marked hearing deficiency, which petitioners concede, to wit: That John is totally deaf in his right ear and that he has a 50% loss of hearing in his left ear. This hearing problem has existed from birth. He wears a hearing aid in his left ear. . . .

By reason of this hearing deficit, Dr. Samuels determined that John should not be permitted to play football, lacrosse or soccer. He rationalized that John's hearing deficit leaves him with a permanent "auditory blind" right side and a diminished sound perception of his left side, even with the use of the hearing aid, and that "this inability to directionalize the source of sound leaves him at increased risk of bodily harm as compared with students with full sensory perception."

In reaching the conclusion that John should not be permitted to play such contact sports, Dr. Samuels, among other things, took into consideration guidelines published by the American Medical Association, Revised Edition 1972, ...

Petitioners contend, however, that Dr. Samuels had not taken into consideration other factors which should have been weighed in his evaluation, such as: that both parents had given their unqualified consent to John's participation in these sports; that John is an all-around athlete of unusual and extraordinary talent; that John has demonstrated his ability to participate extensively in contact sports with his peers who had no hearing disability and that he had never sustained any injury during such competition; that he has actually played football with non-school organizations under the strict supervision of organized athletic groups; and furthermore, that the prohibition against participation in these high school sports has had a damaging psychological effect upon this boy in that he has now lost interest in attending school and has been made to feel inferior to and different from the other children in school.

Both parents, it is true, not only joined in this petition, but testified that they were willing to assume the risk of additional injury to their son, even if same resulted in his becoming totally deaf. John's mother testified that another of her children, a daughter, is, in fact, totally deaf and although she would hope that John would not sustain such complete impairment of hearing, she believed that he could "live with it," and that he would, nevertheless, be able to function well "with such a handicap." John's father reiterated these feelings and added that he hoped John would be able to eventually obtain a college football scholarship as this would be of vital importance because of their limited financial resources.

· · · · · · · ·

It is . . . clear that there are at least conflicting views with respect to whether John's participation in contact sports represents a danger to his physical well-being or to the safety of other students with whom he might participate in such games. A determination of an administrative body, made on a rational basis, should not be judicially set aside.

· · · · · · · ·

The Court recognizes the psychological factors involved in the denial to John of the right to participate in contact sports and, indeed, has great concern for and sympathy with his plight. However, the medical determination of Dr. Samuels, the Court finds, was a valid exercise of judgment and was not arbitrary or capricious since: (a) there exists the risk of danger of injury to the ear in which there is only partial hearing and to which further injury could result in irreversible and permanent damage—in this case, total deafness; (b) aside from the risk of injury to his partially good ear, there also exists the possibility of injury to other parts of John's body by reason of his failure to perceive the direction of sound; and (c) there is the possibility of risk of injury to other participants. Even though these risks may all be minimal, in this Court's opinion it is sound judgment for the school district to follow the advice of its own medical director and the AMA Guide and prohibit John from participating in contact sports.

Respondent is entitled to judgment in its favor dismissing this proceeding.

Note on *Colombo*. A good argument can be made that *Colombo* was wrongly decided and that a court today, more sensitive to the issue of discrimination against handicapped people, would overturn the school district. Technically, this case is not a torts case at all but rather a constitutional law case dealing with the power of the state to regulate. It is useful, however, to briefly consider the problem in a torts context. What tort cause of action, if any, would be available to Colombo? Malpractice? Intentional interference with prospective economic advantage?

A CASE STUDY—*WALTON v. COOK*

[The following complaint and answer are from the case file.

Bill Walton, plaintiff, versus Robert D. Cook and Oregon City Orthopedic Clinic, P.C., an Oregon professional corporation, in a second amended complaint for personal injuries.]

Plaintiff complains of Defendants, and each of them, and for a cause of action alleges:

I. At all times herein mentioned, the Defendant, OREGON CITY ORTHOPEDIC CLINIC, P.C., was, and now is, a business organization, which business organization was at all times herein doing business in the State of Oregon.

II. At all times herein mentioned, Defendant ROBERT D. COOK was a duly licensed physician and surgeon, and was engaged in the practice of medicine in the State of Oregon.

III. At all times herein mentioned, the Defendants, and each of them, were the agents, servants and employees, each of the other, individually and collectively, and were acting within the course and scope of their agency, service and employment.

IV. At all times herein mentioned, Plaintiff was, and continued to be, a medical patient of the Defendants ROBERT D. COOK and OREGON CITY ORTHOPEDIC CLINIC, P.C., and each of them, in the City of Portland, County of Multnomah, and from time to time in Clackamas County, State of Oregon. Said Defendants undertook to examine and treat, and to prescribe for, care for, diagnose for and provide medical care and attention for Plaintiff.

V. From February 28, 1978, until July, 1978, the Defendant OREGON CITY ORTHOPEDIC CLINIC, P.C., and its employee and agent, Defendant ROBERT D. COOK, carelessly and negligently examined, diagnosed, treated, tested and cared for the Plaintiff in the following particulars:

1. In failing to diagnose the development and the eventual fracture of the tarsal navicular bone of the left foot at sometime between mid-February, 1978 and April 22, 1978. At this time, the Plaintiff has been unable to ascertain from his doctors the exact date within that period that the fracture occurred. The Plaintiff complained to Defendant DR. COOK of pain and discomfort in the left foot on the occasions that he visited his office on March 28, 1978, and April 20, 1978, and nearly every day from March 28, 1978, until April 22, 1978, when Plaintiff had contact with Defendant DR. COOK at Portland Trailblazers' practices and games, and Plaintiff's apartment, in the City of Portland, and at the Defendant DR. COOK'S home, in Clackamas County. Additionally, Defendant DR. COOK failed to diagnose said fracture on April 21, 1978, when Plaintiff's left foot was x-rayed at Good Samaritan Hospital, in the City of Portland.

2. The Defendant DR. COOK prescribed oral doses of Butazolidin and Decadron during the period between February 28, 1978, and April 22, 1978, to be taken on a daily basis. On March 28, 1978, at the Memorial Coliseum, the Plaintiff's left foot received four injections of a mixture of Xylocaine and Decadron. On April 20, 1978, in the Defendant DR. COOK'S offices, the Plaintiff received three injections in his left foot of Xylocaine and another drug, which Plaintiff believed to be a corticosteroid. On April 21, 1978, at the Memorial Coliseum, in the City of Portland, the Plaintiff's left foot was injected twice with Xylocaine and a corticosteroid. Said medications were prescribed, administered and injected by Defendant DR. COOK, and constituted wrongful and negligent therapy for Plaintiff's left foot condition.

3. Between March 28, 1978, and April 22, 1978, the Defendant DR. COOK daily recommended and encouraged Plaintiff to bear weight on his left foot and attempt to use it in connection with engaging in basketball practice sessions, and professional basketball games for the Portland Trailblazers. Said recommendations were made both in Clackamas County, at DR. COOK'S office and home, and in Multnomah County at Plaintiff's apartment, the location of the Portland Trailblazer's practice sessions and the Memorial Coliseum. On April 20, 1978, following the aforesaid three injections on Plaintiff's left foot at DR. COOK'S office, DR. COOK recommended that Plaintiff place weight on and exercise his left foot, and on April 21, 1978, at the Memorial Coliseum, Defendant DR. COOK gave Plaintiff medical clearance to participate in a professional basketball game following two injections of Xylocaine and a corticosteroid which had caused Plaintiff's left foot to become numb. The prescription and encouragement of the conduct and activity described above constituted negligent treatment.

4. Following the diagnosis of Plaintiff's left tarsal navicular fracture and at the time of removal of Plaintiff's case on June 2, 1978, at the offices of DR. COOK, Plaintiff was negligently encouraged to resume weight-bearing on his left foot.

VI. As a direct and proximate result of the carelessness and negligence of Defendants described above, Plaintiff suffered a fracture of his left tarsal navicular bone, aggravation of said fracture, lengthening of his disability, permanent weakening of his left foot, increased vulnerability to subsequent fractures of the same and adjoining bones, and damage to the adjoining nerves, muscles and soft tissues of the left foot. As a further proximate result of the carelessness and negligence of the Defendants, Plaintiff has been deprived of his ability to engage in his professional basketball career, which resulted in substantial loss of future earning capacity.

VII. By reason of the premises, it became necessary for Plaintiff to incur expenses for doctors, hospitals, x-ray technicians, travel and other services required in the care and treatment of said injuries that were not paid for by a third party in the amount of $7,500.00.

VIII. By reason of the premises, Plaintiff has been unable to follow his regular employment, to his special damage in a sum of $624,500.00 as of December 16, 1980. Said loss is continuing and thus not yet fully determined.

IX. The Plaintiff remained under the medical care of Defendants ROBERT D. COOK and OREGON CITY ORTHOPEDIC CLINIC, P.C., from February 28, 1978, and into July, 1978. During said period, he relied on the medical advice of the Defendants, and was not informed of the true nature and extent of his injury to his left foot and its negligent cause. The Plaintiff did not discover the nature and extent of his injury to his left foot and its negligent cause until July, 1978, when he began consulting other doctors.

X. By reason of the premises, Plaintiff has been generally damaged in the sum of $5,000,000.00.

WHEREFORE, Plaintiff prays judgment against Defendants, and each of them, jointly and severally, as follows:

1. For general damages in the sum of $5,000,000.00;
2. For special damages in the sum of $632,000.00;
3. For costs and disbursements incurred herein.

· · · · · · · ·

[What follows is the amended answer to the plaintiff's second amended complaint.]

DEFENDANTS, for answer to Plaintiff's Second Amended Complaint, admit, deny and allege as follows:

I. ADMIT that the Oregon City Orthopedic Clinic, P.C., does business in the State of Oregon and that defendant Robert D. Cook is a duly licensed physician and surgeon engaged in the practice of medicine in the State of Oregon, and that he provided medical services to the plaintiff from time to time between February and July, 1978; but defendants deny that they were negligent as alleged in said complaint and deny each and every other allegation contained therein and the whole thereof.

· · · · · · · ·

III. THE injury complained of was caused by Plaintiff's own conduct in one or more of the following respects:

1. In failing to follow the instructions of the defendant physicians and in failing to use proper care for his own welfare;
2. Plaintiff, aware of the risks made an informed judgment to receive the medication, and play, and any claimed injury attributed thereto resulted from his voluntary decision to do so.

WHEREFORE, Defendants pray judgment herein.

Discussion

Although Walton's complaint does not mention the fact, Dr. Cook was employed by the Portland Trailblazers as its team physician. In a supplemental answer to the complaint, Cook contended that Walton was therefore limited to his worker's compensation remedy since he was injured in the course of employment by a co-employee. Viewed in this light, the case is paradigm. Assuming for purposes of discussion that Walton's allegations are true, how is the case likely to be resolved?

To begin, the worker's compensation defense raised by Cook would most likely be unavailing. Cook is likely to be viewed as an independent contractor and not as an employee of the Portland Trailblazers. Of course, more facts would be needed concerning the precise relationship between Cook and the Trailblazers. But in the absence of a showing that Cook was virtually on the working staff of the team, the team physician, in most situations, will probably be viewed as being an independent contractor. Thus, Walton retains his common law tort action against Cook. (Related worker's compensation problems are dealt with in more depth in Chapter 6.)

Walton's allegations of medical negligence run the gamut. His first allegation is negligence in the failure to diagnose the fracture. The reasonableness of Cook's care would be measured against the minimum common skill of orthopedic specialists. As is often the case in professional malpractice, the components of reasonable care will be established through testimony of expert witnesses. In Walton's case, a battle of the experts is foreseeable. The plaintiff's experts would no doubt testify that a reasonably prudent orthopedist would have made the diagnosis. The defendant's experts would testify that such fractures are difficult to discern and that an orthopedist possessing the minimum common skill of members of the profession would not have made the diagnosis. An additional issue would be raised concerning whether Cook should be held to the perhaps higher standard of one with a specialty in sports medicine. This would appear to be a legal issue. Whatever the standard to which Cook is held, it would seem that a jury issue is presented as to whether Cook met the requisite standard of care.

The allegation that Cook negligently prescribed drugs would be evaluated in a similar fashion. Here, the plaintiff would also argue that Cook's decision to prescribe these drugs was influenced, wrongfully, by pressure from the team to have Walton play. Similarly, Cook's decision to permit Walton to play, and to "clear" him for participation, was the negligent by-product of pressure from the team. Once again, the jury's evaluation of Cook's care would be made in light of expert testimony geared to show what a reasonably prudent orthopedist (or sports medicine specialist) would have done.

Finally, Walton alleged that Cook failed to provide him with information concerning the true nature and extent of the injury. The issue here would be whether the reasonably prudent practitioner, possessing the minimum common skill of members in good standing of the profession, would have informed Walton more fully. If in fact Walton was not adequately informed, Cook's defense that Walton made his own decision to play—and thus assumed the risk—would be unavailing. These issues would be likely to go to the jury.

Walton's case was settled before trial for an undisclosed sum.

ADDITIONAL NOTES

1. *Sports injuries and medical malpractice.* As might be expected, a number of medical malpractice cases arise out of injuries incurred in sports. For example, in *Foster v. Englewood and Hospital Association*, 19 Ill. App. 3d 1055, 313 N.E.2d 255 (1974), plaintiff was injured in a neighborhood football game and died during routine surgery. Affirming a trial court judgment in favor of the plaintiff, the court held the hospital, the surgeon, and the anesthetist liable for the death. In this category of cases, general medical malpractice principles apply.

2. In *Speed v. State*, 240 N.W.2d 901 (Iowa 1976), the plaintiff, a University of Iowa basketball player, brought a medical malpractice action alleging that doctors at the university hospital negligently failed to diagnose Speed's intracranial infection and that this resulted in Speed's blindness. The court affirmed the trial court judgment in Speed's favor, applying well-established medical malpractice rules.

3. Negligence might be found due to inadequate emergency medical services. *Fish*, a case discussed in note 5 of Chapter 2, is a good example of such a case.

4. *The recurring issue of vicarious liability.* In almost all of the cases in this chapter, vicarious liability has been an issue. More specifically, the issue raised is whether the doctor is properly viewed as an independent contractor (in which case there is generally no vicarious liability imposed on the employer) or an employee (in which case vicarious liability is imposed for torts committed in the scope of employment). in *Cramer v. Hoffman*, 390 F.2d 19 (2d Cir. 1968), the court held that the university doctor was an independent contractor whose negligence could not be imputed to the university. (Cramer was a college football player who was paralyzed after making a tackle during practice.)

The distinction between an independent contractor and an employee is not particularly clear. Restatement § 220 provides in part:

(2) In determining whether one acting for another is a servant or an independent contractor, the following matters of fact, among others, are considered:

(a) the extent of control which, by the agreement, the master may exercise over the details of the work;

(b) whether or not the one employed is engaged in a distinct occupation or business;

(c) the kind of occupation, with reference to whether, in the locality, the work is usually done under the direction of the employer or by a specialist without supervision;

(d) the skill required in the particular occupation;

(e) whether the employer or the workman supplies the instrumentalities, tools, and the place of work for the person doing the work;

(f) the length of time for which the person is employed;

(g) the method of payment, whether by the time or by the job;

(h) whether or not the work is a part of the regular business of the employer;

(i) whether or not the parties believe they are creating the relation of master and servant; and

(j) whether the principal is or is not in business.

One might well question whether the Restatement guidelines are particularly helpful. Courts appear to be preoccupied with the "control" issue. Prosser believes that "it is probably no very inaccurate summary of the whole matter to say that the person employed is a servant when, in the eyes of the community, he would be regarded as a part of the employer's working staff, and not otherwise" at 460.

5. Another recurring problem is one raised in *Walton* concerning the duty of the team physician to provide information to players concerning the consequences of using pain killing drugs. In a case settled in 1976, it was reported that the Chicago Bears agreed to pay Dick Butkus $600,000. Butkus claimed that extensive injections of cortisone irreparably damaged his knee and that he had not been advised of the long-term effects (New York Times, Sept. 14, 1976, at 50, col. 5).

6. *The statute of limitations problem. Bayless v. Philadelphia National League Club*, 579 F.2d 37 (3rd Cir. 1978), raised an issue similar to that in *Walton*. In *Bayless*, a former pitcher sued the club alleging that the team physician negligently administered painkilling drugs which resulted in his permanent disability. The trial court granted the club's motion for a summary judgment based on the statute of limitations. On appeal, the court reversed and remanded, holding that the statute of limitations begins to run from the time plaintiff knew or reasonably should have known the cause of injury, and not from the time the drugs were administered. Moreover, the court pointed out that the determination of when the statute began to run was a question for the jury. This is in line with the modern view that in medical malpractice cases the statute of limitations will begin to run only when the plaintiff would reasonably have discovered the damage.

BIBLIOGRAPHY

"Aftermath of a Tragedy—Liability of the New York State Athletic Commission for Injuries Suffered in a Prizefight," 14 SYRACUSE LAW REVIEW 79 (1962).

King, J. H., "The Duty and Standard of Care for Team Physicians," 18 HOUSTON LAW REVIEW 657 (1981).

"The Malpractice Liability of Company Physicians," 53 INDIANA LAW JOURNAL 585 (1978).

"Malpractice on the Sidelines: Developing a Standard of Care for Team Sports Physicians," 2 JOURNAL OF COMEDY & ENTERTAINMENT LAW 579 (1980).

Redfearn, Richard W., "The Physician's Role in School Sports Programs," Physician & Sports Medicine, September 1980, at 67.

4

Products Liability for Defective Athletic Equipment

It is not entirely fanciful to suggest that the demise of football as we know it will come about not from a lack of general interest but as a consequence of an economic truth—companies cannot make money manufacturing and selling football helmets. Products liability judgments received by seriously injured football players against helmet manufacturers make the sport of football an endangered species. Helmet manufacturers, saddled with huge and numerous products liability judgments, will pass on these costs to consumers. We may reach the point where football is simply too expensive to play. This chapter explores the legal theories available to sports participants injured by arguably defective sports equipment.

Generally, a person injured by an arguably defective, commercially supplied product has available at least three separate and distinct causes of action—negligence, breach of implied warranty, and strict liability in tort. In some cases, a fourth cause of action, a breach of an express warranty, is available.

The negligence cause of action in the products liability context is not much different from any other negligence-based cause of action. Manufacturers and sellers of products, like all others in the society, generally have a duty to act as reasonably prudent people would act under the same or similar circumstances. In the products liability setting, negligence typically takes one of three forms. One recurring form of negligence pertains to quality control. In this regard, an unreasonable failure to inspect for defects or to test the product is alleged. A second recurring form of negligence is that the design of the product is unreasonably unsafe. A third basis for showing negligent conduct is the manner in which the product is marketed. Here, the likely allegation is that there is a negligent failure to warn about dangers associated with the use of the product. Contributory negligence and assumption of risk are, of course, available as defenses, as they would be for any other negligence-based cause of action.

Under the Uniform Commercial Code, a warranty of merchantability accompanies the sale of goods by a merchant. This warranty assures that the goods are "of fair average quality" and "fit for the ordinary purposes for which such goods are used." (UCC 2–314). Additionally, a warranty of fitness for a particular purpose is created if the buyer relies on the seller's judgment to furnish goods for a special purpose even if the seller is not a merchant. (UCC 2–315). Under the UCC, such warranties may be disclaimed by the seller or lost by the buyer who fails to notify the seller of the breach within a reasonable time. (UCC 2–317 and 2–607). Moreover, assumption of risk, misuse of the product, and failure to follow directions can defeat a breach of warranty claim. Finally, it should be noted that the UCC does not extend the warranty to all those who might foreseeably be expected to be affected by the goods. Rather, the UCC defines the classes of person to whom the warranty extends in three alternate versions of UCC 2–318. Under the version adopted in most jurisdictions, the seller is liable for personal injuries "to his buyer, members of his buyer's family, and guests in his buyer's home." (UCC 2–318, Alternative A).

Both the UCC and the Restatement recognize the availability of causes of action based on express representations made concerning the nature or quality of the product. The UCC addresses the issue in terms of breach of an express warranty under 2–313. The Restatement addresses it under the rubric of tort misrepresentation in section 402B. The gist of each action is similar. The plaintiff must show a misrepresentation of a material fact regarding the nature or quality of the product which causes injury. Assumption of risk and misuse of the product are defenses to both causes of action. It should be noted, however, that under the Restatement, a commercial supplier is liable for injury to anyone who relied on the misrepresentation. Under the UCC, the injured person need not have relied on the express warranty. Instead, the UCC defines the classes of protected persons under the 2–318 alternatives previously mentioned.

Under the theory of strict liability in tort, a commercial supplier who sells a product "in a defective condition unreasonably dangerous to the user or consumer" is subject to liability for harm caused (Restatement § 402A). Liability attaches even if the seller has exercised all possible care and even though the user or consumer has no contractual relation with the seller. The determination of whether a product is defective is made with reference to what a reasonable consumer would expect. Assumption of risk and misuse of the product are defenses.

The cases that follow illustrate more fully the nature of the various products liability causes of action and how such causes of action operate in regard to sports products.

THE LANDMARK CASES

NEGLIGENCE

McCormick v. Lowe & Campbell Athletic Goods Co.
144 S.W.2d 866 (Mo. Ct. App. 1940)

[The defendant, Lowe & Campbell Athletic Goods Company, supplied a vaulting pole which broke while the plaintiff, a high-school pole vaulter, was using it in vaulting. The plaintiff was seriously injured in the subsequent fall and brought a negligence-based cause of action to recover for his injuries. More specifically, the plaintiff alleged that the company was negligent in its failure to inspect and test the pole.

At trial, the plaintiff introduced expert testimony which tended to show that a reasonable inspection would have revealed that the pole was brittle and susceptible to snapping off. The defendant's witness, an employee of the defendant, testified that he customarily tested a pole to make sure it would hold the person for whom it was intended by throwing his weight upon the pole in four different positions. The plaintiff prevailed at trial. The defendant appealed.]

From an examination of the numerous cases cited in the briefs relating to the so-called modern rule governing liability of a manufacturer in cases such as the present one, we conclude that a manufacturer of a product is under a duty to exercise ordinary care to test the product to determine whether or not it has a defect which would render it unsafe when applied to its intended use; that a failure to perform such duty renders the manufacturer liable to a person injured in consequence of such failure while using such article in the ordinary and usual manner. [Citations omitted.]

. . . .

The defendant insists . . . that its evidence "demonstrates" the pole was inspected and tested. There was evidence to the effect the pole "snapped off." This was sufficient . . . to enable the jury to find the pole brittle. The only evidence which it can be said tended to show the pole which broke was tested, was that of the defendant's employee, who stated the manner in which he customarily tested bamboo vaulting poles. . . .

Plainly, the court cannot say such a method of testing was a reasonably careful method. The question was one for the trier of the fact.

Defendant, in contending no case was made for the jury, says the plaintiff failed to prove any act or omission on its part was the proximate cause of his injuries; that plaintiff was guilty of contributory negligence "and had assumed the risk incident" to engaging in pole vaulting.

The facts stated above were sufficient to warrant the jury in finding . . . that if defendant had tested it in a reasonably careful manner the defect would have been discovered and the injury averted. Thus the failure of the defendant to properly test the pole was the direct cause of the accident.

Plaintiff assumed the ordinary risk of pole vaulting but he did not assume risks due to the negligence of the defendant. He did not, prior to the accident, know or have cause to believe the pole was not a safe one to use in vaulting. He vaulted . . . in the usual and skillful manner. This was not negligence as a matter of law. . . .

· · · · · · · ·

The judgment . . . is affirmed.

Dudley Sports Co. v. Schmitt
279 N.E.2d 266 (Ind. Ct. App. 1972)

[Danville High School purchased an automatic baseball-pitching machine from Em-Roe Sporting Goods Company that carried the name, Dudley Sports Company. The machine was manufactured by Commercial Mechanisms, Inc., but marketed by Dudley. Upon receipt of the machine by the high school, the vice principal, Gibbs, and the baseball coach, Trotter, uncrated it. The crate contained a parts list, assembly instructions, and a tag warning that the operation of the machine should be understood before uncrating. The tag referred to operating instructions, but no operating instructions were provided.

Gibbs and Trotter uncrated the machine, assembled it, and used it. It was then placed in a storage room. Schmitt, a student at the school, was severely injured when he was struck by the pitching arm as he swept out the storage room.

Schmitt brought an action against the high school, Em-Roe, and Dudley. In the suit against Dudley, which is the focus of our concern here, Schmitt alleged negligence in the design and manufacture of the machine. Schmitt won a $35,000 judgment at the trial level. Dudley appealed.]

· · · · · · · ·

It is our opinion that a vendor who holds himself out as the manufacturer of a product and labels the product as such must be held to the same standard of care as if he were in fact the manufacturer.

· · · · · · · ·

The reason for imposing such liability is not hard to find. When a vendor puts his name exclusively on a product, in no way indicating that it is the product of another, the public is induced to believe that the vendor was the manufacturer of the product. This belief causes the public to rely upon the skill of the vendor. When products are held out in this manner, the ultimate purchaser has no available means of ascertaining who is the true manufacturer. By this act of concealment, the vendor vouches for the product and assumes the manufacturer's responsibility as his own.

· · · · · · · ·

It is our opinion that the evidence most favorable to Schmitt was sufficient for the jury to conclude that Dudley was negligent in the design, manufacture, and sale of the machine.

Point A.

Schmitt contends that Dudley was negligent for failing to provide a shield around the pitching arm; for failing to provide a lock or catch mechanism on the machine by which the pitching arm could be locked; and for failing to give specific instructions as to the operation of the machine. Dudley replies that a manufacturer is under no duty to design an accident-proof product; that their duty was limited only to the use of reasonable care; that the danger from the lack of a protective shield around the throwing arm was an obvious danger, and therefore no warning was necessary.

While we recognize the validity of the argument that a manufacturer may not be liable for obvious dangers, it is also the law that a manufacturer and vendor are bound to avoid *hidden defects or concealed dangers* in their products. [Citations omitted.]

The lack of a guard around the arm was probably obvious to all potential users of the machine. But the extent of the hazards involved from the lack of a guard was not apparent. The potential risks of harm to the users of this machine lie first in its ability to deliver a swift, crippling blow even though unplugged. Secondly, whether connected or disconnected, if the throwing arm is in the ten o'clock position, a slight vibration or even a change in atmospheric conditions will trigger the throwing arm. This ability to operate while unplugged as a result of even a slight vibration is a latent danger which could only be discovered through an examination of the machine combined with knowledge of the engineering principles which produce the action of the machine. Such knowledge is not ordinarily possessed by a sixteen-year-old high school boy who had never seen the machine before.

In spite of these concealed dangers Dudley asserts that placing a screen around the throwing arm would create a false sense of security, thereby attracting curious persons to place their fingers inside the screen. We are not persuaded by this argument. The utilization of such a protective screen would, in fact, be actual notice of the danger. Those placing their fingers inside the screen would do so at their own risk, as would one who touches the blade of a power saw. Without a screen, however, there is no notice of, or protection from, the inherent dangers of this machine. As a result, the false sense of security is created when there is no screen.

· · · · · · · ·

Point B.

The law requires a supplier of an imminently dangerous chattel to *warn all who may come in contact* with the chattel of any concealed danger, regardless of privity of contract. [Citation omitted.]

Although a manufacturer or vendor is under no duty to warn of apparent dangers, this court has adopted the rule of *Campo v. Scofield* (1950), 301 N.Y. 468, 95 N.E.2d 802, which held that: " . . . in cases dealing with a manufacturer's liability for injuries to remote users, the stress has always been upon the duty of guarding against *hidden* defects and of giving notice of concealed *dangers*." [Citations omitted.]

Dudley argues that because a general warning tag was sent to the High School, no liability can be attached to Dudley for Schmitt's injuries. Dudley did include a general warning tag in the shipping crate warning the High School to read the operating instructions before using the machine. However, this general warning tag hardly conveyed an implication that the machine would only be dangerous when in operation. No warning was given of the latent dangers of this machine. Nothing was mentioned about its triggering capabilities while unplugged. Thus, a more specific warning was required to fulfill Dudley's duty to warn.

The specific operating instructions referred to by the general warning tag were not included in the crate. Presumably, such instructions would have informed the purchaser as to the various positions of the throwing arm, the positions which were dangerous, that the machine was capable of being triggered even though unplugged, and that triggering the machine only required a slight vibration or change in atmospheric conditions.

· · · · · · · ·

Although a manufacturer may assume that the purchaser will properly use the product and avoid obvious dangers, such reliance is improper if the product contains latent dangers and no notice is given thereof. Because no specific operating instructions were sent to the High

School and no warning was given as to the specific latent dangers of the machine, it was reasonably foreseeable that a high school student might be the victim of such negligence. Thus, it was reasonable for the jury to find from the evidence before them that Schmitt's injuries were the natural and probable consequence of Dudley's negligence. [Citations omitted.]

There is no vitality in Dudley's argument that the machine was in keeping with modern scientific advancement in the baseball pitching machine industry and that it was an advancement when compared to the other models on the market. The fact that a particular product meets or exceeds the requirements of its industry is not conclusive proof that the product is reasonably safe. In fact, standards set by an entire industry can be found negligently low if they fail to meet the test of reasonableness. [Citations omitted.]

· · · · · · · ·

The jury could well have found that Dudley violated its duty to notify the High School, and ultimately Schmitt, of the machine's inherent dangers.

· · · · · · · ·

The decision of the trial court is therefore affirmed.

MISREPRESENTATION AND BREACH OF WARRANTY

Hauter v. Zogarts
14 Cal. 3d. 104, 534 P.2d 377, 128 Cal. Rptr. 681 (1975)

[The defendant manufactures and sells the "Golfing Gizmo"—a device designed to improve one's golf swing. The defendant marketed the Gizmo as a "completely equipped backyard driving range" which would permit the user to "drive the ball with full power." According to the defendant, the Gizmo was: "COMPLETELY SAFE BALL WILL NOT HIT PLAYER." Essentially, the Gizmo consisted of a golf ball attached to an elasticized cord secured to the ground by metal pegs.

Louise Hauter purchased a Gizmo from the defendant and gave it to her 13-year-old son, Fred, as a Christmas gift. Fred suffered permanent brain damage when he was struck on the head by the golf ball on the Gizmo. Causes of action were brought in Fred's name alleging false representation, strict liability in tort, and breaches of express and implied warranties. The jury returned a verdict for the defendant on each cause of action. The trial judge granted the plaintiff's motion for judgment notwithstanding the verdict. The defendant appealed. The court here affirmed. What follows is that portion of the opinion dealing with the false representation and warranty causes of action.]

Plaintiff's claim of false representation relies on common law tort principles reflected in section 402B of the Restatement Second of Torts. [Footnote omitted.] For plaintiffs to recover under this section, defendants' statement "COMPLETELY SAFE BALL WILL NOT HIT PLAYER" must be a misrepresentation of material fact upon which plaintiffs justifiably relied. (Rest. 2d Torts, § 402B, coms. f, g, and j.)

If defendants' assertion of safety is merely a statement of opinion—mere "puffing"—they cannot be held liable for its falsity. [Citation and footnote omitted.] Defendant's statement is so broad, however, that it properly falls within the ambit of section 402B. The assertion that the Gizmo is completely safe, that the ball will not hit the player, does not indicate seller's subjective opinion about the merits of his product but rather factually describes an important characteristic of the product. Courts have consistently held similar promises of safety to be representations of fact.

These decisions evidence the trend toward narrowing the scope of "puffing" and expanding the liability that flows from broad statements of manufacturers as to the quality of their products. [Footnote omitted.] Courts have come to construe unqualified statements such as the instant one liberally in favor of injured consumers. [Footnote omitted.] Furthermore, the illustrations in the Restatement indicate that the assertion "COMPLETELY SAFE BALL WILL NOT HIT PLAYER" constitutes a factual representation. Defendants' statement parallels that of an automobile dealer who asserts that the windshield of a car is "shatterproof." [Citations omitted.]

Moreover, the materiality of defendants' representation can hardly be questioned; anyone learning to play golf naturally searches for a product that enables him to learn safely. Fred Hauter's testimony that he was impressed with the safety of the item demonstrates the importance of defendants' statement. That Fred's injury occurred while he used the Gizmo as instructed proves the inaccuracy of the assertion on the carton.

Defendants, however, maintain that plaintiffs' reliance upon the assurance of safety is not justifiable. (See Rest. 2d Torts, § 402B, com. j.) Alluding to the danger inherent to the sport, defendants argue that the Gizmo is a "completely safe" training device only when the ball is hit squarely. Defendants repeatedly state that an improperly hit golf shot exposes the player, as well as others nearby, to a serious risk of harm; they point to testimony recounting how an experienced player once hit a shot so poorly that the ball flew between his legs. As a result, contend defendants, plaintiffs cannot reasonably expect the Gizmo to be "completely safe" under all circumstances, particularly those in which the player hits beneath the ball.

Defendant's argument does not withstand analysis. Fred Hauter was not "playing golf." He was home on his front lawn *learning* to play the game with the aid of defendants' supposedly danger-free training device. By practicing in an open, isolated area apart from other golfers and free of objects off which a poorly hit shot could ricochet, Fred Hauter *eliminated* most of the dangers present during a normal round of play. Moreover, even though certain dangers are inherent in playing golf, the risk that the golfer's own ball will wrap itself around his club and strike the golfer on the follow-through is not among those dangers. Fred Hauter's injury stemmed from a risk inherent in defendants' product, not a risk inherent in the game of golf.

Additionally, defendants' analysis would render their representation of safety illusory. Were we to adopt their analysis, the words "COMPLETELY SAFE BALL WILL NOT HIT PLAYER" would afford protection to consumers only in *relatively infrequent instances* in which the "duffers" using the Gizmo managed to hit the ball solidly. Yet defendants' instructions supplied with the Gizmo clearly indicate the defendants anticipated the users of their product would "hook," "slice" and "top" the ball. They expected their customers to commit the errors that normally plague beginning golfers. Thus, when they declared their product "completely safe," the only reasonable inference is that the Gizmo was a safe training device for all golfers regardless of ability and regardless of how squarely they hit the ball.

Although defendants claim they did not intend their statement to cover situations such as the one at bar, subjective intent is irrelevant. The question is not what a seller intended, but what the consumer reasonably believed. The rule "is one of strict liability for physical harm to the consumer, resulting from a misrepresentation of the character or quality of the chattel sold, even though the misrepresentation is an innocent one, and not made fraudulently or negligently." (Rest. 2d Torts, § 402B, com. a.)

We conclude that Fred Hauter reasonably believed he could use the Gizmo with safety and agree with the trial court that plaintiffs established all the elements of a cause of action for misrepresentation.

· · · · · · · ·

Defendants breached their express warranty that the Golfing Gizmo ball was "completely safe" and would "not hit Player," as well as their implied warranty of merchantability.

As an alternative cause of action, plaintiffs claim that defendants breached both an express warranty and an implied warranty of merchantability. [Footnote omitted.] In analyzing these claims, we confront for the first time the California Uniform Commercial Code provisions relating to warranties. (Cal. U. Com. Code, §§ 2313, 2314, and 2316.) The crucial issue here is not whether defendants created a warranty—as explained below, they clearly did. Rather, the bone of contention is whether they can escape liability by impliedly limiting the *scope* of their promise.

We first treat the claim for breach of express warranty, which is governed by California Commercial Code section 2313. [Footnote omitted.] The key under this section is that the seller's statements—whether fact or opinion—must become "part of the basis of the bargain." [Footnote and citations omitted.] According to official comment 3 to the Uniform Commercial Code following section 2313, "no particular reliance . . . need be shown in order to weave [the seller's affirmations of fact] into the fabric of the agreement. Rather, any fact which is to take such affirmations, once made, out of the agreement requires clear affirmative proof."

· · · · · · · ·

The trial court properly concluded . . . that defendants expressly warranted the safety of their product and are liable for Fred Hauter's injuries which resulted from a breach of that warranty.

The trial court also held for plaintiffs on the theory of breach of an implied warranty of merchantability. [Footnote omitted.] Unlike express warranties, which are basically contractual in nature [citation omitted], the implied warranty of merchantability arises by operation of law. [Citation omitted.] "Into every mercantile contract of sale the law inserts a warranty that the goods sold are merchantable, the assumption being that the parties themselves, had they thought of it, would specifically have so agreed." [Citation omitted.] Consequently, defendant's liability for an implied warranty does not depend upon any specific conduct or promise on their part, but instead turns upon whether their product is merchantable under the code. . . .

[T]he evidence shows that the Gizmo is not fit for the ordinary purposes for which goods are normally used.

· · · · · · · ·

Defendants nevertheless seek to avoid liability by limiting the scope of their warranties. They claim that the box containing the Gizmo and the instructions pertaining to its use clarified that the product was "completely safe" only when its user hit the ball properly. They point to no language expressing such a limitation but instead claim that a drawing in the instructions depicting a golfer "correctly" using their product *implies* the limitation.

As we explained above in discussing the false representation claim, defendants' argument is wholly without merit. Furthermore, they fail to meet the stern requirements of California Uniform Commercial Code section 2315 [footnote omitted] which governs disclaimer and modification of warranties. Although section 2316 has drawn criticism for its vagueness, [footnote omitted] its purpose is clear. No warranty, express or implied, can be modified or disclaimed unless a seller *clearly* limits his liability. . . .

Because a disclaimer or modification is inconsistent with an express warranty, words of disclaimer or modification give way to words of warranty unless some clear agreement between the parties dictates the contrary relationship. [Citations omitted.] At the very least, section 2316 allows limitation of warranties only by means of *words* that clearly communicate that a particular risk falls on the buyer. [Footnote omitted.]

Moreover, any disclaimer or modification must be strictly construed against the seller. [Citations omitted.] Although the parties are free to write their own contract [citations omitted], the consumer must be placed on fair notice of any disclaimer or modification of a warranty and must freely agree to the seller's terms. [Citation omitted.] "A unilateral nonwarranty cannot be tacked onto a contract containing a warranty." [Citation omitted.]

In the instant case, defendants do not point to any language or conduct on their part negating their warranties. They refer only to a drawing on the box and to the notion that golf is a dangerous game; based on that meagre foundation, they attempt to limit their explicit promise of safety. Such a showing does not pass muster under the code, which requires clear language from anyone seeking to avoid warranty liability. We conclude, therefore, that the trial court properly granted plaintiffs' judgment notwithstanding the verdict with regard to the warranty causes of action.

STRICT LIABILITY IN TORT

Nissen Trampoline Company v. Terre Haute First National Bank
332 N.E.2d 820 (Ind. Ct. App. 1975)

[The defendant Nissen manufactured the "Aqua Diver"—a small circular trampoline to be used recreationally in lieu of a diving board. Nissen's literature described the Aqua Diver as "twice as much fun as an old fashioned diving board at half the cost." Southlake Beach purchased an Aqua Diver from Nissen and installed it on a platform at its beach.

Thirteen-year-old Bruno Garzolini, Jr., was injured while using the

Aqua Diver at Southlake. The Terre Haute First National Bank, as guardian of Bruno's estate, initiated an action against Nissen and Southlake. Of concern here is the cause of action in strict liability against Nissen.

At trial, Bruno testified that he was injured the first time he used the Aqua Diver when he attempted to jump from the designated platform onto the bed of the trampoline in order to catapult himself into the water. He landed with only one foot on the trampoline. His other foot became entangled in the elastic cables, which supported the bed of the trampoline. He then found himself suspended by his left leg, which was ensnarled in the cables. Eventually, Bruno's left leg had to be amputated above the knee. Other evidence at trial revealed that Nissen was aware that a user's foot could become dangerously entangled in the cables supporting the bed of the trampoline. The product was marketed without any warnings or instructions for use.

The trial court jury returned a verdict for Nissen. The trial judge granted a new trial, pointing out that the jury verdict was against the weight of the evidence, which supported plaintiff's strict liability claim. Nissen appealed. The court here affirms the award of a new trial.]

· · · · · · · ·

Initially, Nissen argues that the trial court's conclusion that the Aqua Diver was a defective product was not supported by substantial evidence. Nissen maintains that there was no evidence which established a defect in design or manufacture. . . .

Our analysis of the evidence reveals that, as Nissen maintains, no defect in design or manufacture has been shown. However . . . for reasons hereinafter stated, it is our opinion that . . . defectiveness is predicated upon Nissen's failure to warn of the known dangers in the use of the Aqua Diver.

Under the doctrine of strict tort liability as expressed in Restatement (2d) Torts, § 402A, and adopted in Indiana [citations omitted], it is well established that a product, although virtually faultless in design, material, and workmanship, may nevertheless be deemed defective so as to impose liability upon the manufacturer for physical harm resulting from its use, where the manufacturer fails to discharge a duty to warn or instruct with respect to potential dangers in the use of the product. Generally, the duty to warn arises where the supplier knows or should have known of the danger involved in the use of its product, or where it is unreasonably dangerous to place the product in the hands of a user without a suitable warning. However, where the danger or potentiality of danger is known or should be known to the user, the duty does not attach. [Citations omitted.]

In the case at bar, the trial court's findings, which are supported by uncontradicted evidence, reveal that prior to marketing the Aqua Diver, Nissen had discovered through testing that it was possible for a user's foot to pass between the elastic cables connecting the bed of the trampoline to the circular frame and thereby cause injury. Additionally, the undisputed evidence reveals that notwithstanding the knowledge of this danger involved in the use of Aqua Diver, Nissen marketed the product without a warning. This undisputed evidence . . . is substantial evidence to support the trial court's conclusion that the Aqua Diver was a defective product dangerous to the user without a warning within the purview of § 402A. We therefore conclude that there were sufficient special findings to establish that Aqua Diver was defective. . . .

· · · · · · · ·

Clearly, under the doctrine of strict liability, an essential element of proof is that the defective condition of the product caused plaintiff's harm. . . .

The issue of causation in both negligence and strict liability cases wherein the defect is in design or manufacture differs fundamentally from causation in failure to warn cases. In the former, it is generally required that the plaintiff establish a causal connection in fact by proof that the harm resulted from the condition or ingredient that made the product defective. In the latter case, however, the difference arises in that the factor rendering the product defective is separable from the product itself. Applying the causation in fact test to the failure to warn case would give rise to a doctrine that liability is predicated upon a showing by the plaintiff that he would have suffered no injury but for the absence of warning. Stated differently, the plaintiff would be required to show that he would have heeded a warning had one been given. In our opinion, such an approach would undermine the purpose behind the doctrine of strict tort liability since any such testimony would generally be speculative at best. A more reasonable approach which represents a compromise within the framework of strict liability . . . is that the law should supply the presumption that an adequate warning would have been read and heeded, thereby minimizing the obvious problems of proof of causation. We find such an approach to be meritorious, workable, and desirable.

Comment j of Restatement (2d) Torts § 402A (1965), provides a presumption protecting the manufacturer where a warning is given: "Where warning is given, the seller may reasonably assume that it will be read and heeded; . . . "

However, where there is no warning as in the case at bar, the presumption of comment j that the user would have read and heeded an adequate warning works in favor of the plaintiff user. In other words, the presumption of causation herein is that Garzolini would have read an adequate warning concerning the danger of a user's foot slipping between the elastic cables of Aqua Diver and heeded it, resulting in his not using the Aqua Diver. This presumption may, however, be rebutted by the manufacturer Nissen with contrary evidence that the presumed fact did not exist. As the Texas Supreme Court said in *Technical Chemical Co. v. Jacobs*, 480 S.W.2d 602 (Tex. 1972): "Depending upon the individual facts, this may be accomplished by the manufacturer's producing evidence that the user was blind, illiterate, intoxicated at the time of use, irresponsible or lax in judgment or by some other circumstance tending to show that the improper use was or would have been made regardless of the warning," 480 S.W.2d at 606.

Placing the burden of rebutting the presumption of causation on the manufacturer in failure to warn cases is not inconsistent with the policies behind strict liability. [Footnote omitted.] It would encourage manufacturers to provide safe products and to warn of the known dangers in the use of the product which might cause injury. Such a presumption would also discourage those manufacturers who would rather risk liability than provide a warning which would impair the marketability of the product. [Footnote omitted.] The presumption of causation in failure to warn cases is not to be taken as an abrogation of the issue of causation, thereby subjecting a manufacturer to liability for almost any injury caused by his product. Rather, it merely shifts to the manufacturer the burden of proof where the fact-finder could only speculate as to whether the injury could have been prevented by a warning.

· · · · · · · ·

Judgment affirmed.

THE FOOTBALL HELMET ON TRIAL

When a football player suffers a head or neck injury, is the helmet manufacturer liable? This note explores that question—a question upon which the future of football may well turn.

The Scope of the Problem

Accurate and precise data concerning the incidence of head and neck injuries is unavailable. There is no central registry to compile information about such injuries. In the late 1970s, the National Electronic Injury Surveillance System, which monitors hospitals for the U.S. Consumer Product Safety Commission (CPSC), estimated that about 30,000 of the 318,000 annual football injuries treated in hospital emergency rooms were head and neck injuries. These included subdural hematomas, spinal-cord injuries, fractured cervical vertebrae, nerve-pinch injuries, fracture dislocations, vascular injuries, and severe concussions. Additionally, the CPSC extrapolated that football players suffer approximately 45,000 concussions annually. Estimates vary regarding deaths and serious spinal-cord injuries. National projections from local data, however, would indicate that somewhere in the vicinity of 40 to 50 spinal-cord injuries occur annually, accompanied by perhaps 20 deaths directly attributable each year to participation in football. Not all these consequences, of course, can be linked to the use of the football helmet. Just what role the helmet plays in all this is problematical.

The Role of the Helmet

In the early 1970s, the CPSC commissioned the National Bureau of Standards (NBS) to study the problem of head-injury protection. NBS reported back in a study entitled "Standards for Athletic Helmets—State of the Art and Recommendations." The gist of the report was that no satisfactory performance standards existed. The same is true today. In the absence of performance standards, it is difficult to assess the quality of modern football helmets. A few things, however, must be noted.

The state-of-the-art helmet appears to effectively absorb energy from a blow so as to avoid excessive jolts to the brain. Thus, there is good reason to believe that there has been a reduction in the number of serious brain contusions and concussions. Evidence also exists, however, to support the view that there has been a corresponding increase in spinal-cord injuries. The new helmet technology, in short, may be protecting the head at the expense of the neck.

The modern helmet contains a faceguard. Many observers believe that the faceguard contributes to an increased incidence of cervical injuries by helping to transmit the force of the blow to the cervical area. In some instances, it acts like a lever in snapping the head back. The result is that the often unpadded rear edge of the helmet injures the neck. Thus, many capable observers believe the faceguard should be eliminated entirely or equipped with spring releases similar to those on ski bindings.

Finally, it must be observed, not all helmets in use are "the top of the line." There has never been a recall of obviously inadequate helmets and manufacturers continue to turn out cheaper models.

The manufacturers. In the past decade, the number of helmet manufacturers has declined dramatically. Some, like Spalding and MacGregor, have made the conscious business choice not to manufacture helmets. Others have gone bankrupt. In either case, the cost associated with litigation was a substantial factor in bringing about the result. Riddell, a major remaining manufacturer of football helmets, indicated in 1977 that it might leave the market if tort judgments continued going the way they had been going. Riddell was stunned by a 1975 case in which a Miami, Florida, jury awarded an injured player $5.3 million (*Stead v. Riddell, Inc.*, U.S. Dist. Ct. Fla., No. 74 1520 (Civ.) Dec. 15, 1975).

Sporting-goods industry sources estimated in 1977 that $150 million in lawsuits was pending against helmet manufacturers while the entire business of selling helmets generated $12 million wholesale and $24 million retail. Arthur Young's 1979 audit of Riddell resulted in a "qualified" opinion of the parent company because of the uncertainty surrounding the 30 pending lawsuits against Riddell. In 1982, a Los Angeles jury awarded $3.5 million dollars in damages to quadriplegic Demott Davis. Riddell was the defendant.

The Case Against the Helmet

The modern case against the helmet will typically involve a Restatement § 402A cause of action alleging that the helmet is in a "defective condition unreasonably dangerous" to the player. More specifically, the thrust of the plaintiff's claim is that the helmet has been defectively designed and marketed.

Defective Design. The modern products liability case often revolves around a claim that the product is defectively designed. In such a case, the plaintiff impugns the conscious design choice of the manufacturer and attempts to show a safer, economically feasible design. In determining whether the manufacturer's choice of design renders the product in a "defective condition unreasonably dangerous," courts have been unable to agree on a single standard. In one of the clearer statements of the applicable principles, the Supreme Court of Texas, in *Turner v. General Motors Corp.*, 584 S.W.2d 844 (Tex. 1979), decided in favor of considering the following factors:

> 1. The utility of the product to the user and to the public as a whole weighed against the gravity and likelihood of injury from its use;
>
> 2. The availability of a substitute product which would meet the same need and not be unsafe or unreasonably expensive;
>
> 3. The manufacturers' ability to eliminate the unsafe character of the product without seriously impairing its usefulness or significantly increasing its costs;
>
> 4. The user's anticipated awareness of the dangers inherent in the product and their avoidability because of general public knowledge of the obvious condition of the product, or of the existence of suitable warnings or instructions (584 S.W.2d at 846).

Two concurring justices pointed out that the proper test was whether the product "was dangerous to an extent beyond that which would be contemplated by the ordinary consumer who purchases it with the ordinary knowledge common to the community as to its characteristics" (584 S.W.2d at 854).

Depending on the facts of a particular case, a helmet might be regarded as being defectively designed on a number of different theories. First, it may be that the helmet did not adequately absorb energy from the blow. A player suffering a brain injury would be the likely plaintiff in such a case. State-of-the-art helmet shells would be the standard by which to measure the helmet here. Plaintiffs suffering cervical injuries are likely to allege that the helmet is in a "defective condition unreasonably dangerous" because its design protects the head at the expense of the neck. In this regard, it should be pointed out that the NBS report alluded to earlier viewed this as an undesirable design choice—concussions, after all, are greatly preferred over paralysis. The cervically injured plaintiff would also attack the faceguard. No matter what the theory, the substance of the plaintiff's claim is that, given the availability of economically feasible safer alternatives and in light of the consumer's expectation in regard to safety, the helmet design is unreasonably dangerous.

Defective marketing. Failure to provide adequate instructions or warnings can also support the contention that the product, as marketed, is defective. In a similar fashion, failure to recall might render a product defective. Case law also supports the view that "overpromotion" or overzealous marketing could provide the grist for a section 402A claim. Thus, such a cause of action should at least be considered against the helmet manufacturer.

In Defense of the Helmet

The manufacturer will of course deny the existence of the elements of the plaintiff's case. One recurring allegation will be that, even if the helmet is defective, the defect did not in fact cause the harm. That is to say, the harm would have occurred even if the helmet was defect-free. Additionally, the manufacturer will argue a lack of proximate cause—pointing out both the unforeseeability of the result and the intervening acts (such as bad coaching or faulty training practices) which supersede and cut off the liability of the manufacturer. And of course the manufacturer will contest the issue of the helmet's defectiveness.

Invariably the manufacturer will also claim that the plaintiff is precluded from recovery because of assumption of risk or misuse of the product. For assumption of risk defense to be effective, the defendant must ordinarily show that the plaintiff in fact recognized the specific danger associated with his use of the product but nevertheless voluntarily chose to expose himself to it. Although it is fair to say that football players assume certain risks of injury, it is not clear that they voluntarily assume the known risks associated with defective helmets. In order for misuse to operate as a defense, the defendant must ordinarily show that the use was not reasonably foreseeable. Assuming the player is injured in the course of play, it is difficult to see how a misuse defense can be successfully argued. "Spearing," for example, would be a foreseeable misuse.

The future of the helmet. At the outset of this chapter, it was noted that it was not entirely fanciful to suggest that the demise of football was a possible consequence of the helmet litigation. One additional thought—this would surely be a healthy development. The neutral application of our established legal principles would appear to increase the likelihood that the manufacturers will be asked to pay the freight. The fact that this cannot be profitably accomplished bespeaks the fact that football as we know it is really socially undesirable. Perhaps the invisible hand of the free market is simply assisting us in drawing that conclusion.

ADDITIONAL NOTES

1. *The negligence-based cause of action.* In *Filler v. Rayex Corp.*, 435 F.2d 336 (7th Cir. 1970), a manufacturer of sunglasses which shattered when struck by a baseball, causing the loss of the player's eye, was liable for negligent failure to warn users of the dangers of its product. Compare the result in *James v. Hillerick & Bradsby Company, Inc.*, 299 S.W.2d 92 (Ky. 1957), in which a pitcher was struck by a piece of a baseball bat which had broken off when the batter swung. In denying recovery, the court pointed out that even though the bat may have been defective, the company was not negligent:

It is our opinion that the ordinary risks of personal injury included in a baseball . . . game, from the breaking of even a properly made bat are such that a defective bat cannot be said . . . to create an "unreasonable risk." It is common knowledge that bats frequently break, and we think it is immaterial that a properly made bat ordinarily will splinter with the grain while one made of defective wood may break across the grain. The risk of injury is not materially increased by the defect. (*Id.* at 94)

Weistart and Lowell note that the result in *James* "may be subject to considerable question" (at 1000).

A recurring issue in the negligence cases concerns the effect of an intervening cause on the original tortfeasor's liability. For example, in *Dudley*, the defendant alleged that Gibbs and Trotter were negligent in failing to store the baseball-pitching machine under lock and key and that their negligence superseded or cut off the liability of Dudley. This is a proximate cause issue. The court in *Dudley* correctly decided the issue, pointing out that, generally, an intervening act of negligence does not cut off the liability of the original wrongdoer: "Where harmful consequences are brought about by intervening . . . forces, the operation of which should have been foreseen, the chain of causation extending from the original wrongful act to the injury is not broken by the intervening . . . force. The original wrongful act will still be treated as the proximate cause of the accident" (*Id.* at 276).

In *Fort Lauderdale Country Club v. Winnemore*, 189 So.2d 222 (Fla. Dist. Ct. App. 1966), the plaintiff was injured when he was struck by a golf cart driven by his companion and provided by the country club. In his suit against the country club, the plaintiff contended that the cart was negligently maintained. The club contended that the negligent driving of the plaintiff's companion was the sole legal cause of the injuries. In affirming the plaintiff's judgment, the court noted that the conduct of the driver, even if negligent, "was not an intervening cause which breaks the chain of causation" (*Id.* at 224). According to well-established tort principles, *Dudley* and *Fort Lauderdale* were correctly decided. As a general rule, intervening acts of negligence do not supersede or cut off the liability of the original wrongdoer. Courts view such acts as foreseeable. On the other hand, intervening acts, which can be characterized as grossly negligent, or intentional, ordinarily do supersede and cut off the liability of the wrongdoer. Thus, if Dudley's companion was drunk while driving the cart, a better case could be made that the country club was not liable.

2. *The warranty-based causes of action*. It should be remembered that a breach of warranty cause of action is by nature contractual. Therefore, privity of contract is an issue. The traditional common law rule was that the plaintiff must have entered into some contractual relationship with the defendant in order to have a cause of action for breach of warranty. The matter is now largely governed by the UCC, which defines classes of people protected in three alternative versions of 2–318. Under Alternative A, the seller is liable for personal injuries to his buyer, members of his buyer's household, and guests in his buyer's home. As already noted, Alternative A has been adopted in most jurisdictions. Alternatives B and C provide broader warranties. Alternative B provides that a warranty extends to any natural person who could be expected to use, consume, or be affected by the goods and who is injured in person by the breach. Alternative C extends liability even further in that it covers property damage and is not confined to natural persons.

If the gravamen of the complaint is based on a misrepresentation, the cause of action sounds in tort. Under the Restatement § 402B, a commercial seller is potentially liable to anyone who relies on the misrepresentation. Privity of contract is not an issue in the misrepresentation cause of action. In theory there is no liability for misrepresentation if the plaintiff has not relied on it.

3. *The strict liability in tort cause of action.* As previously noted, Restatement § 402A requires that the plaintiff show that the product was in a "defective condition unreasonably dangerous." In 1972, the California Supreme Court rejected the requirement that the plaintiff prove that the defect was "unreasonably dangerous" in *Cronin v. J.B.E. Olson Corp.*, 8 Cal. 3d 121, 104 Cal. Rptr. 433, 501 P.2d 1153 (1972). The overwhelming majority of jurisdictions, however, adhere to the Restatement approach that the product must be both defective and unreasonably dangerous.

The determination of whether a product is in a defective condition unreasonably dangerous is made with reference to what a reasonable consumer would expect. By way of illustration, a cherry pie with a cherry pit in it would not be regarded as in a defective condition unreasonably dangerous. The reasonable consumer would expect to find a pit in a cherry pie every now and then. A review of the case law reveals that there are three basic types of defects—manufacturing flaws, design flaws, and marketing flaws. Manufacturing flaws can be described as individualized product imperfections. An example would be a coffee roll with a pebble in it. Design flaws impugn the entire product line. In litigation concerning the Ford Pinto, it was contended that all the Pintos of a given year were defective because Ford placed the gas tank in a dangerously vulnerable position behind the rear axle. This would be an example of an alleged design defect. Finally, marketing flaws arise when the seller fails to provide needed instructions regarding proper use, or to provide adequate warnings concerning not-so-obvious dangers. The Aqua Diver described in *Nissen* would be in this category.

4. It can be argued that a number of commonly used sports products are in defective conditions unreasonably dangerous to the user or consumer. The cases in this chapter dealt with a baseball-pitching machine, a golf-training machine, a vaulting pole, a football helmet, and a trampoline. There are reported cases dealing with baseball glasses, shotgun shells, ski boats, swimming pools, golf carts, snowmobiles, motorcycles, pool tables, bicycles, and elastic exercisers. Although there may be no reported cases, Astro Turf and its kissing cousins—Poly Turf and Tartan Turf—appear to be susceptible to attack on a products liability theory. New technologies make wooden bats and noncollapsible rims suspect. Baseball helmets without ear flaps and mouth guards are arguably defective. The point is that the possibilities are infinite. In any sports-related accident, a products liability suit which puts the sports equipment under scrutiny should at least be considered.

5. *Artificial turf litigation.* One of the most controversial issues in the

sports arena today is whether artificial turf should continue to be used as a playing surface. Coaches and trainers report numerous artificial turf-related injuries including heat strokes and exhaustion, turf toe (i.e., sprained great toe), concussions, ankle and knee injuries, first- and second-degree burns, secondary infections, blisters, and dehydration. Despite these injuries, the use of artificial turf has been justified because it results in an increase in the players' speed, lowers maintenance costs, and increases use of the playing facilities.

As of this writing, there has been no litigation of this actual issue. But athletes are suing increasingly for injuries resulting from a defective product, so such a suit is likely to occur in the near future. If a player does decide to bring a products liability suit, he may have a cause of action under the theories of (1) negligence, (2) breach of warranty, and/or (3) strict liability.

Under a negligence theory, those responsible for the decision to use artificial turf could be held liable for an athlete's injuries for breach of duty to exercise reasonable care for the athlete's protection. Team owners, stadium owners, universities, and colleges could be found negligent for breaching their duties to provide protection against any unreasonable risk of harm to the athlete. Finally, a manufacturer might be negligent for failing to exercise reasonable care in the manufacture and sale of the turf.

Warranty theories may be premised on two separate grounds. Manufacturers of artificial turf create an express warranty if they tell buyers that the turf is "safer than grass." An athlete who relies on this statement and is then injured may sue the manufacturer for breach of an express warranty. Athletes may also have a cause of action for breach of an implied warranty if artificial turf is not suitable for the purpose for which it is sold.

Finally, a manufacturer is subject to a charge of strict liability for developing and selling a product that is unreasonably dangerous because of a defective condition. If the athlete is injured, the doctrine applies even if the manufacturer is not negligent.

BIBLIOGRAPHY

Epstein, Robert K., "The Case Against Artificial Turf," 13 TRIAL, January 1977, at 42.

Mandel, Bernard, "Negligent Design of Sports Facilities," 16 CLEVELAND-MARSHALL LAW REVIEW 275 (1967).

Peters, George A., "Unsafe Swimming Pools and Spas Claim Unsuspecting Victims," 16 TRIAL, March 1980, at 42.

Philo, Harry M. & Stine, Gregory, "The Liability Path to Safer Helmets," 13
      TRIAL, January 1977, at 38.
Troy, F. E., "In Defense of Artificial Turf," 13 TRIAL, January 1977, at 46.
Wilkinson, Allen P., "Sports Product Liability: It's All Part of the Game—Or Is
      It?," 17 TRIAL, November 1981, at 58.

5

Defamation and Invasion of Privacy

Defamation

The rules governing liability for defamation make about as much sense as the rules governing the conjugation of irregular verbs in French. What follows is an attempt to present, as clearly as possible, a picture of the current rules.

Profile of the Tort of Defamation at Common Law: The Plaintiff's Prima Facie Case—A Strict Liability Tort

The tort of defamation, as it existed at common law, can be defined as the unconsented to and unprivileged intentional communication to a third person of a false statement about the plaintiff which tends to harm the reputation of the plaintiff in the eyes of the community. Consent and privilege are affirmative defenses that must be pleaded and proved by the defendant. Once defamatory meaning is apparent, injury to reputation is generally presumed as a matter of law. Moreover, the plaintiff is given the benefit of a rebuttable presumption that the statement is false, thus making truth a defense to be pleaded and proved by the defendant. Therefore, the plaintiff's prima facie case consists of a simple allegation that the defendant intentionally communicated to a third person a statement about the plaintiff which tended to expose the plaintiff to such things as public hatred, shame, obloquy, contumely, odium, contempt, ridicule, aversion, ostracism, degradation, or disgrace.

It should be noted that the tort of defamation is in substance one of strict liability. That is to say, the only intent that is required is the intent to communicate something to a third person. In the vast majority of cases, of course, the defendant clearly intends to communicate something to a third person even though she may not intend to defame or harm the plaintiff. In fact, it appears that the only type of case in which the courts are willing to concede that the requisite intent to communicate is lacking involves situations, for example, in which the defendant is alone with the plaintiff, defaming her to her face, and an unanticipated intruder overhears the defamatory utterance.

As to all other matters which conceivably could be either intended or negligently performed, the defendant is strictly accountable. It thus makes absolutely no difference that the defendant *does not intend* to lie, defame, or harm the plaintiff. Likewise, it is immaterial that the defendant *does not negligently* lie, defame, or harm the plaintiff. The defamer, in short, is strictly liable for whatever she intentionally communicates to a third person about the plaintiff if it turns out that what she said is false, injures the plaintiff's reputation in the eyes of the community, and is neither consented to by the plaintiff nor privileged. At common law, people communicate virtually at their own peril. The printed and written word is, in a legal sense, indistinguishable from nitroglycerin and dangerous animals—if someone is hurt by use of it, liability attaches.

The Libel/Slander Per Se/Per Quod Distinctions

Common law defamation consists of the two torts of libel and slander. Libel is written or printed defamation—defamation embodied in some tangible or permanent form and therefore generally subject to wide dissemination. Slander is oral defamation—fleeting and ephemeral and therefore generally not subject to wide dissemination. Any libel which is clearly defamatory, with no need to resort to extrinsic facts to show the defamatory meaning, is said to be actionable per se. The phrase "actionable per se" means that general damage to reputation will be presumed. Slander is actionable per se only if the slanderer says that the plaintiff (1) committed a crime of moral turpitude, (2) has venereal disease or something equally loathsome and communicable, (3) is somehow unfit or not to be trusted in his or her occupation, or (4) is not chaste.

A libel that is not actionable per se is actionable per quod. The phrase "actionable per quod" means that there is no presumption of general damage to reputation and that the plaintiff must plead and prove "special damages," usually of a pecuniary nature. Libel per quod exists when the defamatory statement is innocent on its face but takes on a defamatory meaning when illuminated by proof of extrinsic facts. The extrinsic facts had to be pleaded by way of "inducement," "innuendo," or "colloquium." If the defamatory meaning could be established only by reference to facts not apparent on the face of the publication, the plaintiff had to show such facts by way of "inducement." The purpose of the requirement called "innuendo" was to explain the meaning of the words in light of the facts. So, for example, a false statement that the plaintiff had given birth to twins was not defamatory on its face since there was nothing there that would hold the plaintiff up to scorn or ridicule; but when it was pleaded by way of inducement that she was married one week at the time of the birth and by way of innuendo (for the slow to catch on) that she must have had premarital intercourse, a defamatory statement was made out. Libel per quod, however, can be magically transformed to libel per se if it turns out that the defamatory statement as illuminated by extrinsic facts falls within one of the four classes of slander actionable per se. Slander which does not fall into one of the four categories is only actionable per quod.

The requirement that the plaintiff plead and prove special pecuniary damages in cases which are only actionable per quod often proves to be a difficult obstacle to overcome. If, however, the plaintiff is successful in showing special pecuniary damage, general damages are then appropriate for presumed reputational injury along with nonpecuniary special damages, such as emotional distress or physical illness.

Available Defenses

Truth. Assuming that the plaintiff has made out a prima facie case, the defendant may escape liability by establishing that what was communicated was true or was either absolutely or conditionally privileged. Truth is a complete defense if the defendant can show that the imputation is substantially true. Generally, the defendant need not show literal truth but must establish that what was communicated was basically true as to the "sting" of the libel. Truth is generally a total defense regardless of the motives. Belief as to truth, however honest it may be, is no justification for defamation.

Privilege. Privilege, like truth, is a complete defense if it is established by the defendant. The rationale for the existence of privilege as a defense is that conduct which may otherwise impose liability is excusable if the defendant is acting in furtherance of some socially useful interest. That is to say, it is more desirable, from a social standpoint, to protect the defendant and allow the plaintiff to go uncompensated. If an absolute privilege is found to exist, the defendant is totally immune from liability. Absolute privilege arises when the defendant is acting in furtherance of some very important social interest—an interest so important that the court is willing to immunize the defendant from liability for false statements without regard to purpose, motive, or reasonableness. Absolute privilege is confined to the few situations where there are obvious strong policy reasons in favor of permitting unbridled speech. Thus, statements made in the course of the judicial or legislative proceedings are absolutely privileged. Executive communications, arguably made in the discharge of official duties, are likewise absolutely privileged. The media are absolutely privileged for defamation uttered by political candidates who have been granted equal time under the Federal Communications Act.

Qualified privilege. The most common defense involves a claim of qualified privilege, which arises when the defendant is arguably justified in talking. It is somewhat difficult to define qualified privilege with any degree of precision; the cases reveal repeated reliance on Baron Parke's formulation that a statement is privileged when it is "fairly made by a person in the discharge of some public and private duty, whether legal or moral, or in the conduct of one's own affairs in matters where his interest is concerned." (See, e.g., *Watt v. Longsdon*, [1930] 1 K.B. 130.) The immunity conferred on the defendant is conditioned on his or her good behavior; the defendant must act properly or else the privilege is defeated. In general, a qualified privilege is defeated by the existence of facts inconsistent with the purpose of the privilege. The common law qualified privilege includes the privilege to fairly comment on matters of public concern by offering opinion, but not false statement of fact, and to fairly and accurately report public proceedings.

The Matrix of Relevant Supreme Court Cases

New York Times Co. v. Sullivan
376 U.S. 254 (1964)

In March of 1960, L. B. Sullivan was one of three elected commissioners to the city of Montgomery, Alabama. As such, he supervised the Montgomery police department, fire department, department of cemetery, and department of scales. On March 29, 1960, the *New York Times* ran a full-page advertisement entitled "Heed Their Rising Voices." The advertisement stated that thousands of Southern blacks, engaged in a nonviolent effort to secure constitutionally protected rights, were being met by an "unprecedented wave of terror," perpetuated by "Southern Violators," designed to prevent them from enjoying their constitutional rights. The Montgomery police were implicated on a number of occasions as "Southern Violators."

It was uncontroverted that some statements in the advertisement were not accurate descriptions of events which occurred in Montgomery. The text of the advertisement concluded with an appeal for funds and appeared over the names of 64 persons—many widely known for accomplishments in religion, public affairs, trade unions, and the performing arts. L. B. Sullivan sued the *New York Times* and four black Alabama clergymen who signed the advertisement. A Montgomery County jury found that Sullivan was defamed and awarded him a half million dollars, the full amount claimed, against all the defendants. The Alabama Supreme Court affirmed, and the Supreme Court granted certiorari "because of the importance of the Constitutional issues involved."

Although the Alabama law that was applied in *New York Times* did not differ significantly from the common law already described, the Supreme Court, with Justice Brennan writing the majority opinion, held "that the rule of law applied by the Alabama Courts is constitutionally deficient for failure to provide the safeguards for freedom of speech and of the press that are required by the First and Fourteenth Amendments in a libel action brought by a public official against critics of his official conduct." The Court went on to say that the evidence presented in the case was "constitutionally insufficient" to support the judgment for the respondent. The common law then, according to the Supreme Court, was inherently constitutionally defective.

The Supreme Court considered the *New York Times* case "*against* the background of a profound national commitment to the principle that debate on public issues should be uninhibited, robust and wide-open, and that it may well include vehement, caustic and sometimes unpleasantly sharp attacks on government and public officials." The Court quoted Judge Learned Hand to the effect that the first amendment "presupposes that right conclusions are more likely to be gathered out of a multitude of tongues than through any kind of authoritative selection" and that although "[t]o many this is . . . folly," we have, nonetheless, as a society, "staked upon it our all." In view of this national commitment to robust, wide-open debate, Justice Brennan reasoned "that erroneous statement is inevitable in free debate and that it must be protected if the freedoms of expression are to have the 'breathing space' that they 'need . . . to survive.' " Brennan cited Judge Edgerton for the simple truth that "whatever is added to the field of libel is taken from the field of free debate."

The Court then constructed legal rules to ensure that our national commitment was not compromised. According to the Court, the Constitution requires "a federal rule that prohibits a public official from recovering damages for a defamatory falsehood related to his official conduct unless he proves that the statement was made with 'actual malice'— that is, with knowledge that it was false or with reckless disregard of whether it was false or not." Moreover, the aggrieved official must prove "actual malice" with "convincing clarity"—a standard of proof which is arguably more demanding than proof by a mere preponderance of evidence.

Thus was born the constitutional privilege in defamation cases. The original and exclusive owner of the privilege, it should be noted, was the "citizen critic" of government.

Curtis Publishing Co. v. Butts and Its Companion, *Associated Press v. Walker*
388 U.S. 130 (1967)

Three years after the landmark *New York Times* decision, a majority of the Supreme Court agreed to extend the constitutional privilege to defamatory criticism of "public figures." Although Justice Harlan announced the results in both *Butts* and *Walker*, a majority of the Court agreed with Chief Justice Warren's conclusion in his concurring opinion that the *New York Times* test would apply to criticism of "public figures" in addition to "public officials." The Court's extension of the constitutional privilege to defamatory criticism of public figures made the *New York Times* privilege available to those who defamed people "intimately involved in the resolution of important public questions" or who "by reason of their fame, shape events in areas of concern to society at large."

The *Butts* case originated with an article in the *Saturday Evening Post* accusing Wally Butts of conspiring to "fix" a football game between the University of Georgia and the University of Alabama. At the time of the article, Butts was the athletic director of the University of Georgia. The article accused Butts of giving team secrets to the opposition. Butts brought a libel action in federal court against Curtis Publishing Company, the publisher of the *Saturday Evening Post*, seeking $5,000,000 compensatory and $5,000,000 punitive damages. At trial, the defendant relied on the defense of truth. The jury returned a verdict for $60,000 in general damages and $3,000,000 in punitive damages. The court reduced the total award to $460,000 by remittitur. The Court of Appeals for the Fifth Circuit affirmed, and the Supreme Court granted certiorari and affirmed the decision.

Walker, the companion case to *Butts*, arose out of the distribution of a news story giving an eyewitness account of events on the campus of the University of Mississippi on the night of the infamous riot which erupted as a consequence of federal efforts to enforce a judicial decree ordering the enrollment of James Meredith as the first black student at the university. The story stated that General Walker, a retired career soldier and staunch segregationist, personally led a charge against the federal marshalls' attempt to carry out the court order. Walker sued the Associated Press in the Texas state courts and asked for $2,000,000 in compensatory and punitive damages. Walker denied taking part in any "charge" against federal officials. Although the Associated Press defended on the basis of truth, a verdict of $500,000 compensatory damages and $300,000 punitive damages was returned. The trial judge, however, refused to enter the punitive award on the ground that there was no evidence of "actual malice." Both sides appealed, and the Texas Court of Civil Appeals affirmed. After the Supreme Court of Texas denied a writ of error, the Supreme Court of the United States granted certiorari and reversed.

The rationale used by the Chief Justice in his concurring opinion was that "differentiation between 'public figures' and 'public officials' . . . has no basis in law, logic or First Amendment policy." The same test should apply both to the public figure plaintiff and public official plaintiff; each must show "actual malice" in order to recover. "[W]alker was a public man in whose public conduct society and the press had a legitimate and substantial interest." Because he did not prove actual malice, Walker could not recover. Butts, too, was a public figure; but unlike Walker, Butts proved "actual malice," because the jury's punitive damage award was preceded by an instruction that such an award was appropriate only if "actual malice" was found. Butts, then, could recover. The result is that the privilege which once belonged only to the citizen critic of government is extended to the citizen critic of the public person.

Rosenbloom v. Metromedia, Inc.
403 U.S. 29 (1971)

Approximately four years after *Butts* and *Walker*, the Supreme Court took the *New York Times* privilege one logical step further. Justice Brennan, writing for the plurality, concluded in *Rosenbloom* that the *New York Times* protection should extend to defamatory falsehoods relating to private persons, if the statements concerned matters of general or public interest.

George Rosenbloom was a distributor of "nudist magazines" in the Philadelphia metropolitan area. During an obscenity crackdown, he was arrested for selling allegedly obscene material as he was making a delivery to a retail dealer. A few days after the arrest, the police obtained a search warrant to search Rosenbloom's home and warehouse and seized Rosenbloom's allegedly obscene inventory. Rosenbloom, who by this time was out on bail, was again arrested. Following the second arrest, a Metromedia, Inc., radio broadcast included an item about Rosenbloom. The report broadcast stated that obscene materials had been confiscated at Rosenbloom's home.

Rosenbloom then sued various city and police officials and several local news media alleging that the material seized was not obscene. Rosenbloom asked for injunctive relief prohibiting further police harassment as well as further publicity of the arrests. Metromedia, in turn, reported that "girlie book peddlers" in the "smut literature racket" were seeking judicial relief. Rosenbloom, however, was not mentioned by name. Rosenbloom subsequently was acquitted of the criminal obscenity charge on the grounds that his magazines were not obscene. Following the acquittal, he filed a libel suit in federal district court, alleging that Metromedia's unqualified characterizations of his books as "obscene" and of him as a "girlie book peddler" in the "smut literature racket" were defamatory and constituted libel per se.

At trial, Metromedia's defenses were truth and privilege. After receiving instructions which did not apply the *New York Times* privilege, but clearly articulated common law rules, the jury returned a verdict for Rosenbloom and awarded him $25,000 in general damages and $725,000 in punitive damages. The trial court then reduced the punitive damage award to $250,000 on remittitur. The Court of Appeals for the Third Circuit reversed, holding that judgment be entered for Metromedia because Rosenbloom's evidence did not reasonably support the conclusion that Metromedia had acted with "actual malice" as constitutionally defined. The Supreme Court granted certiorari and affirmed the judgment of the court of appeals.

In affirming the lower appellate court, the Supreme Court in *Rosenbloom* extended the constitutional privilege to protect defamatory falsehoods concerning "private persons" if the statements concerned matters of "general or public interest." The Court focused on society's interest in learning about certain issues: "If a matter is a subject of public or general interest, it cannot suddenly become less so merely because a private individual is involved, or because in some sense the individual did not 'voluntarily' choose to become involved." "Private individuals involved in an event of public interest" are the legal equivalents of "public officials" and "public figures." All have to prove "actual malice" to recover in a defamation action.

The Court went on to carefully analyze the role of the free press, the public's right to know, and the importance of the first amendment, concluding that the constitutional protection extended "to all discussion and communication involving matters of public or general concern, without regard to whether the persons involved are famous or anonymous." The critical inquiry concerns the subject matter of the discussion.

Gertz v. Robert Welch, Inc.
418 U.S. 323 (1974)

By 1974, hundreds of post–*New York Times* defamation cases had been before the courts. The result of this avalanche of litigation was a continuing struggle to find the appropriate balance between the rights of free speech and press and the right to be free from character attacks.

In *Gertz v. Robert Welch, Inc.*, the Supreme Court reversed the trend by severely limiting, if not overruling, *Rosenbloom*.

In 1968, a Chicago policeman named Nuccio shot and killed a youth named Nelson. The policeman was subsequently found guilty of second degree murder by state prosecutors. The Nelson family retained Elmer Gertz to represent them in civil litigation against Nuccio.

Robert Welch published *American Opinion*, a monthly periodical of the John Birch Society. The magazine had long warned of a nationwide conspiracy to discredit local law enforcement agencies and create a national police force supporting a communist dictatorship. As a part of his effort to alert the public, Welch commissioned and published an article on the policeman's murder trial. In the article, Gertz was portrayed as a communist official with a criminal record. Statements made in the article contained serious factual inaccuracies.

Gertz filed an action for libel in the United States District Court for the Northern District of Illinois, alleging injury to his reputation as a lawyer and citizen. Welch claimed that he was entitled to the constitutional privilege and asked for summary judgment on the grounds that Gertz would not be able to show "actual malice." The court denied the motion, concluding that Gertz might be able to prove "actual malice." After all the evidence was heard, the district court ruled that Gertz was not a public figure or public official and therefore did not have to prove "actual malice" to recover. The case was submitted to the jury, and the jury determined that the appropriate measure of damages was $50,000.

Following the jury verdict and on further reflection, the district court entered judgment for the defendant notwithstanding the verdict, anticipating the *Rosenbloom* decision. The district court concluded that discussion of a public issue was constitutionally protected, that Welch's statements pertained to a public issue, and that Gertz had not met the *New York Times* "actual malice" standard. The *Rosenbloom* decision intervened, and the United States Court of Appeals for the Seventh Circuit then agreed with the district court and affirmed its judgment, citing *Rosenbloom*. The United States Supreme Court granted certiorari to reconsider the extent of a publisher's constitutional privilege against liability for defamation of a private citizen and reversed.

The Supreme Court in *Gertz* carefully reviewed the development of the law of defamation through *New York Times* and *Rosenbloom* in light of the competing interests of free speech and press and of protecting an individual's reputation. The Court recognized the critical importance of free speech and press to robust debate; the Court also recognized that "absolute protection for the communications media would require a total sacrifice of the competing value served by the law of defamation," and that the "legitimate state interest underlying the law of libel is the compensation of individuals for the harm inflicted on them by defamatory falsehood." Balancing the interests, the Court concluded that the protection afforded the media under *Rosenbloom* was too broad: "[T]he extension of the *New York Times* test proposed by the *Rosenbloom* plurality would abridge this legitimate state interest to a degree that we find unacceptable."

Thus the "public or general interest" test for determining the applicability of the *New York Times* standard was rejected as inadequately serving the competing values at stake. The Supreme Court concluded that the states should retain substantial latitude in their efforts to fashion a remedy for defamatory falsehoods about private individuals and that so long as liability was not imposed without fault, the states could define for themselves the appropriate standard of liability.

To guard against the states using their new latitude to intrude upon the first amendment, the Court then stated the requirement that state-proscribed remedies "reach no farther than is necessary to protect the legitimate interest involved" and concluded that "[i]t is necessary to restrict defamation plaintiffs who do not prove knowledge of falsity or reckless disregard for the truth to compensation for actual injury." Thus, presumed or punitive damages cannot be recovered by the private plaintiff who establishes liability under a less demanding standard than *New York Times*.

The Court then turned its attention to the continuing dilemma of the "public person" as plaintiff. The *Gertz* Court endorsed its prior decisions in *Butts* and *Walker* and sought to further define the status of a public figure. Under *Gertz*, a public figure designation may rest on either of two alternatives:

In some instances an individual may achieve such pervasive fame or notoriety that he becomes a public figure for all purposes and in all contexts. More commonly, an individual voluntarily injects himself or is drawn into a particular public controversy and thereby becomes a public figure for a limited range of issues. In either case such persons assume special prominence in the resolution of public questions.

For the second category—public people for a limited range of issues—it "[i]s preferable to reduce the public-figure question to a more meaningful context by looking to the nature and extent of an individual's participation in the particular controversy giving rise to the defamation." Public people in general enjoy "significantly greater access to the 'channels' of effective communication and hence have a more realistic opportunity to counteract false statements than private individuals normally enjoy." They typically also "invite attention and comment." In contrast, "private individuals are not only more vulnerable to injury than public officials and public figures; they are also more deserving of recovery."

The Court concluded that Gertz was a private person and that the *New York Times* standard was not applicable. Because the jury was allowed to impose liability without fault and was permitted to presume damages without proof of actual injury, a new trial was ordered by the court.

Time, Inc. v. Firestone
424 U.S. 448 (1976)

Less than two years later, in 1976, the Supreme Court added yet another link to the chain of defamation cases that began twelve years earlier with *New York Times v. Sullivan*. This time the Court was called on to refine its definition of "public figure."

In 1964, Mary Alice Firestone and Russell Firestone sought the dissolution of their marriage in Florida. Since Russell was heir to one of America's wealthiest industrial fortunes, the proceeding drew a great deal of attention in the Miami press. After judgment in the divorce proceeding was rendered, *Time* magazine printed an item under its "Milestones" section, which stated that Russell Firestone had been granted a divorce on the grounds of extreme cruelty and adultery. The article characterized the marriage as having "enough extramarital adventures on both sides to make Dr. Freud's hair curl."

Within a few weeks of publication, Mary Alice Firestone demanded a retraction from *Time*. When the magazine refused, a libel action was commenced against it in Florida circuit court. A jury ultimately awarded Ms. Firestone $100,000 in damages. The decision was reviewed by the Florida District Court of Appeals and ultimately affirmed by the Florida Supreme Court. The United States Supreme Court granted certiorari in 1975.

Time, Inc., contended that as a publisher it was entitled to the *New York Times* conditional privilege and thus could not be found liable unless it was established that the article was published with "actual malice." In support of this contention, *Time* argued that Ms. Firestone was a "public figure" and that the proceeding was of "a class of subject matter which . . . deserves the protection of the 'actual malice' standard." The Supreme Court rejected both propositions.

The Court applied the *Gertz* criteria for defining a public figure and found that Ms. Firestone did not attain this status: "[r]espondent did not assume any role of especial prominence in the affairs of society . . . and she did not thrust herself to the forefront of any particular public controversy." The Court explained that Ms. Firestone did not voluntarily enter the public spotlight or freely choose to publicize issues concerning her married life. She had to use the courts to obtain a divorce.

Time's attempt to "equate 'public controversy' with all controversies of interest to the public" failed. The Court noted that "[w]ere we to accept this reasoning, we would reinstate the doctrine advanced in the plurality opinion in *Rosenbloom v. Metromedia, Inc.*"

Despite the fact that the *Firestone* Court rejected the argument that the *New York Times* privilege should extend to the *Time* publisher, the Court nevertheless refused to affirm the Florida court and remanded the case for readjudication. The Court noted that the record did not indicate evidence of fault on the part of the defendant charged with publishing the defamatory material. Since "*Gertz* established . . . that not only must there be evidence to support an award of compensatory damages, there must also be evidence of some fault on the part of a defendant," the Court had no choice but to remand for further proceedings.

The Common Law after *Firestone*

Gertz fundamentally altered the common law. As Justice White remarked, "[l]est there be any mistake about it, the changes wrought by the Court's decision cut very deeply." No area of the common law was left unaffected. The most important lines of delineation are public plaintiffs and private plaintiffs. It may also be important to distinguish media from nonmedia defendants. A consideration of the possible litigant combinations reveals the rough outline of the new rules.

Gertz makes it clear that a public person suing a mass media defendant must show "actual malice" to recover. *Gertz* also makes it clear that a private person suing a mass media defendant must show fault and actual injury to recover. But because of the ambiguity in *Gertz*, a public plaintiff suing a nonmedia defendant doesn't know what he or she has to prove to recover. It is simply not clear whether *Gertz* is limited to cases involving media defendants or applies as well to nonmedia speakers.

If *Gertz* is limited to the media, a public person, in particular kinds of suits against a nonmedia speaker, will be entitled to recover on a common law strict liability theory. For example, if a nonmedia defendant speaks privately about the private life of a public person, constitutional limitations on liability are inapposite. If *Gertz* applies to nonmedia speakers, a public person would presumably have to show "actual malice" to recover.

A private person suing a nonmedia defendant faces a similar dilemma. If *Gertz* is limited to the media, the private person is entitled to rely on a common law strict liability theory in suits against nonmedia speakers. If *Gertz* applies to nonmedia speakers, then arguably the private plaintiff must show at least fault and actual injury.

If all of this sounds like so much hocus-pocus, take heart: you are not alone. With the possible exception of the Supreme Court Justices, no one knows what *Gertz* means. A clearer outline of the law of defamation will not be possible until the Court clarifies its approach to defamation problems.

Invasion of Privacy

It is generally accepted that invasion of privacy consists of four separate and distinct causes of action: (1) intrusion, (2) misappropriation, (3) public disclosure of private facts, and (4) "false light" invasion of privacy. All are especially relevant to sports.

The intrusion cause of action is stated when the plaintiff's right to solitude is invaded by the defendant in a manner that would be objectionable to a person of ordinary sensibilities. The classic intruder is the Peeping Tom. Intrusion might take place in the form of constant annoyance or excessive surveillance. Overzealous paparazzi may well be tortious intruders. This kind of intrusion is obviously relevant in sports. In a similar fashion, the overprotective team owner might intrude on a player's solitude in a desire to check on the player's drug habits.

Misappropriation occurs when the plaintiff's name or likeness is used for a primarily commercial advantage without the plaintiff's consent. Thus, marketing a Hank Aaron baseball glove without Hammerin' Hank's permission would be misappropriation. It should be pointed out that the media enjoy a broad privilege to report the news. Thus, photographs and stories in newspapers and magazines are generally not actionable even if they indirectly boost sales. The gist of the tort is a commercially motivated misappropriation.

Perhaps the purest of the privacy torts is the public disclosure of true private facts in a way that offends a person of ordinary sensibilities. This so-called true privacy tort takes place when a disclosure is made of facts that a reasonable person would wish to keep private because of the embarrassment that the disclosure would create. Once again, newsworthiness operates in the manner of a defense. The cause of action may well turn on whether reasonable people agree that a certain piece of private information about a celebrity is newsworthy or not. As can be seen, the tort lacks a clear profile.

The final privacy tort is false light privacy, which occurs when the plaintiff has been placed in a false light in the public eye. This tort is closely related to defamation, and, although the Supreme Court has not entirely settled the issue, it would appear that the defamation rules previously discussed would apply to this tort as well. In fact, false light privacy appears capable of swallowing defamation entirely in that a cause of action is stated for false statements whether they are defamatory or not. Although the statements which place the plaintiff in a false light typically are defamatory, they need not be. For example, in *Spahn v. Julian Messner, Inc.*, 43 Misc. 2d 219, 250 N.Y.S.2d 529 (1964), the plaintiff Spahn was able to recover for false but laudatory statements about him. (The *Spahn* case is one of the landmark cases that follow.) In *Time, Inc. v. Hill*, 385 U.S. 374 (1967), the Supreme Court held that plaintiffs in such cases had to prove actual malice in order to recover.

THE LANDMARK CASES

DEFAMATION

Time, Inc. v. Johnston
448 F.2d 378 (4th Cir. 1971)

DONALD RUSSELL, Circuit Judge

The defendant is the publisher of *Sports Illustrated*, a weekly periodical devoted to sports and athletics. Annually, it features its selection of "Sportsman of the Year." In 1968, it chose Bill Russell, a star on the professional basketball team of the Boston Celtics, as its "Sportsman of the Year" and engaged George Plimpton, a well-known writer, especially in the field of sports, to write the feature article. In developing his article, Plimpton quoted from interviews he had had with persons acquainted with Russell and his exceptional talents as a basketball player. In quoting an interview with Red Auerbach, Russell's coach, Plimpton included in his article the following paragraph:

"That's a word you can use about him—he (Russell) 'destroyed' players. You take Neil Johnston— . . . , Russell destroyed him. He destroyed him psychologically as well, so that he practically ran him out of organized basketball. He blocked so many shots that Johnston began throwing his hook farther and farther from the basket. It was ludicrous, and the guys along the bench began to laugh, maybe in relief that they didn't have to worry about such a guy themselves."

The "Johnston" referred to in the quoted paragraph is the plaintiff. At the time of the incident referred to, he was an outstanding professional basketball player with the Philadelphia Warriors basketball team. He subsequently retired from professional basketball and is now the assistant basketball coach at Wake Forest University in Winston-Salem, North Carolina. Following the publication of the article, he sued the defendant, contending that he had been libeled in the quoted paragraph and had been "damaged in his chosen profession, that of coaching basketball."

After discovery was completed, both parties moved for summary judgment. [Footnote omitted.] The District Court, after argument, denied both motions, 321 F. Supp. 837, and both parties have appealed.

Upon application under Section 1292(b), 28 U.S.C., this Court granted leave to the parties to take an interlocutory cross-appeal.

We reverse the denial of defendant's motion for summary judgment and dismiss plaintiff's cross-appeal.

The defendant invoked, in support of its motion, the constitutional rule of privilege, granted under the First Amendment, as applied in *New York Times Co. v. Sullivan* (1964). . . . [Citation and footnote omitted.]

There can be no dispute that at the time of the events discussed in the challenged publication the plaintiff met the criteria of "a public figure." "Public figures," within the contemplation of the rule in *New York Times*, as enlarged by subsequent cases, are "those persons who, though not public officials, are 'involved in issues in which the public has a justified and important interest' " and "include artists, athletes, business people, dilettantes, anyone who is famous or infamous because of who he is or what he has done." [Footnote omitted.] Consonant with this definition, a college athletic director, a basketball coach, a professional boxer and a professional baseball player, among others, have all been held to be "public figures." [Citations and footnotes omitted.] The plaintiff, as he figures in the challenged publication, fits this definition of a "public figure." . . . He had offered his services to the public as a paid performer and had thereby invited comments on his performance as such. In a sense, he assumed the risk of publicity, good or bad, as the case may be, so far as it concerned his public performance. The publication in question related strictly to his public character. It made no reference to his private life, it involved no intrusion into his private affairs. It dealt entirely with his performance as a professional basketball player; it discussed him in connection with a public event in which the plaintiff as a compensated public figure had taken part voluntarily.

The plaintiff does not seriously question the defendant's premise that he was a "public figure" at the time of the event discussed in the publication; and the District Court apparently assumed in its decision that the plaintiff was such a "public figure." The plaintiff points out, though, that the event, to which the publication related, occurred twelve years before the publication and nine years after the plaintiff had retired as a professional basketball player. It is plaintiff's position that he had, at the time of publication, shed his character of "public figure" and that the *New York Times* standard was, therefore, inapplicable. This is the basic point of difference between the parties on this aspect of the case. The District Court accepted the plaintiff's view. In so doing, it erred.

The District Court relies for its conclusions primarily on a comment set forth in a note in *Rosenblatt v. Baer*, (1966) 383 U.S. 75, 87, 86 S.Ct 669, 677, 15 L. Ed.2d 597, note 14: "To be sure, there may be cases where a person is so far removed from a former position of authority that comment on the manner in which he performed his responsibilities no longer has the interest necessary to justify the *New York Times* rule." This, however, is not such a case as was envisaged by Justice Brennan. The claim that plaintiff had retired as a player in 1958, nine years before the publication, is misleading. While plaintiff did retire as a player in 1958, he, by his own affidavit, "remained in organized professional basketball, until 1966." He thus identifies himself with professional basketball up to approximately two years of the publication in question. And, at the time of the publication itself, he was a college basketball coach, still involved as a public figure in basketball. Perhaps as a college basketball coach, he was not as prominently identified with the sport as in his playing days. Neither was Butts as intimately identified with football as an athletic director as he had been as a coach but that did not make him an anachronism in football history any more than the plaintiff, with his outstanding record, had become a forgotten figure among the many devotees of the game of basketball.

That even the plaintiff did not reckon his career as a professional basketball player forgotten is demonstrated by his claim in this case that a reflection on that career and on his eminence as a player damages him in his present occupation as a college basketball coach. By his claim for damages here, he is contending that his standing as a college basketball coach rests substantially on the public recollection and estimation of his former career as a professional basketball player; and it is for that reason he sues. It is because he is still engaged in basketball and because of the effect that any adverse comment on his record and achievements as a basketball star may have on his present position in basketball that he claims damage herein. It is manifestly inconsistent for him to contend that, when his basis for damage is thus grounded, his "public figure" career has become so obscure and remote that it is no longer a subject of legitimate public interest or comment.

The event to which the publication related remained a matter of public interest not simply because of its relation to plaintiff's own public career; it had an equal or greater interest as marking the spectacular debut of Russell in a career that was still phenomenal at the time of the publication. It was an event that had, in the language of one sports writer reporting it, a "tremendous psychological effect on the league." It was an event that was vivid in the memory of Auerbach at the time of the publication and likely in that of other followers of the sport. It is fair to assume that in the memory of basketball fans, the event described was neither remote nor forgotten; nor was it devoid of newsworthiness.

Moreover, mere passage of time will not necessarily insulate from the application of *New York Times Co. v. Sullivan*, publications relating to the past public conduct of a then "public figure." No rule of repose exists to inhibit speech relating to the public career of a public figure so long as newsworthiness and public interest attach to events in such a public career. This issue of remoteness as providing a basis for casting a veil about "public figures" in "public events" has often arisen in privacy cases. There are, it is true, distinctions between actions for an invasion of privacy and suits for defamation [footnote omitted] but the same considerations it would seem would be present in either case in determining whether mere passage of time will remove the protection afforded by the constitutional privilege created by *New York Times* for a publication relating to a past event in the career of a "public figure."

. . . .

In summary, we conclude that . . . because of plaintiff's classification of a "public figure" . . . the defendant was clearly entitled to invoke the constitutional privilege afforded by the rule in *New York Times Co. v. Sullivan* and related cases.

The plaintiff, by his cross-appeal, however, has raised the point that, even if defendant be entitled to a First Amendment privilege, the motion for summary judgment should have been denied because there was sufficient evidence in the record that the defendant had published the challenged item with actual knowledge of its falsity, or recklessly without regard to whether it was true or not and thereby lost its constitutional privilege. The District Court concluded to the contrary. Recognizing that, if the *New York Times* immunity rule applies, "summary judgment, rather than trial on the merits, is a proper vehicle for affording constitutional protection," where there is no substantive basis for a finding of "knowing falsity or reckless disregard," [footnote omitted] it held "that if the plaintiff were a 'public figure' or if he were otherwise amenable to either standard as set out in *Curtis Publishing Company v. Butts, supra,* he could not, as a matter of law, recover in this action and summary judgment should be granted in favor of the defendant." There is nothing in the affidavits and depositions now before the Court which would give substance to a finding of actual malice, as defined in *New York Times v. Sullivan,* or an extreme departure from the standards of conduct of responsible publishers, as enunciated by Mr. Justice Harlan in *Curtis Publishing Company v. Butts.* [Footnote omitted.] We agree that there is no basis in the record to support a finding of "knowing falsehood or reckless disregard" on the part of the defendant.

It is undisputed that Auerbach, whose statement is quoted in the allegedly offensive statement, was correctly quoted. So long as the press correctly quotes another's statement about a matter of legitimate public interest, does not truncate or distort it in any way, and properly identifies the source, recent decisions indicate that it may properly claim the protection of *New York Times.* [Citations omitted.] It is the plaintiff's contention, however, that the statement of Auerbach, though admittedly made by Auerbach and correctly quoted in the article, was known by the defendant to be false and defamatory and that, because of knowing falsity, the defendant is in no position to claim immunity under the doctrine of *New York Times*. To support such contentions he points to two phrases as being knowingly false and defamatory. These phrases are "destroyed" and "psychologically destroyed," which he argues, taken in the context of the article and giving them their normal connotation, were libellous and were refuted by material in the defendant's own files. Manifestly, the challenged words were not used literally. No one reading the article would have assumed that Auerbach was stating that the plaintiff was actually and literally "destroyed," during the game being discussed. Auerbach was attempting to identify Russell's emergence as a star basketball player; he did that by recounting an event which, as he saw it, marked the beginning of Russell, the star, and incidentally, the eclipse of the plaintiff as star. In describing the event, he used phrases of some vividness, used them in a figurative, not literal, sense, used a form of hyperbole typical in sports parlance. *New York Times*, in its application, does not interdict legitimate or normal hyperbole. [Citation omitted.] To deny to the press the right to use hyperbole, under the threat of removing the protecting mantle of *New York Times*, would condemn the press to an arid, desiccated recital of bare facts. . . . And the records available in the files of the defendant, so far from refuting this opinion that Russell had on the occasion in question "dominated" and outplayed the plaintiff, gave support to that conclusion and provided a rational basis for Auerbach's perhaps vivid characterization. [Citation omitted.] Thus, in an interview with Russell reported earlier in SPORTS ILLUSTRATED Russell himself claimed that he had "psyched" Johnston in this their first encounter. And the comment of both Russell and Auerbach on the rivalry between Russell and the plaintiff on this occasion found confirmation in the account written contemporaneously by the sports reporter of *The New York Times*, an account which was in the files of the defendant. The article put it that, "Basketball fans all over the country buzzed about it (i.e., Russell's 'defensive wizardry') for days afterward." The adjective "psychological" was used both in this article and in other newspaper accounts in describing the impact of Russell's defensive methods on this occasion. There was thus no basis for any conclusion that the defendant was in possession of any fact that would have justified on its part a "high degree of awareness of . . . probable falsity" of the statement made by Auerbach. [Citation omitted.] The District Court was accordingly clearly right in concluding that the record included "nothing . . . which would give substance" to a finding of "knowing falsity or reckless disregard" on the part of the defendant.

Affirmed in part, vacated in part, and remanded with directions that judgment be entered for the defendant.

PRIVACY CASES

Spahn v. Julian Messner, Inc.
43 Misc. 2d 219, 250 N.Y.S.2d 529 (1964)

[Sections 50 and 51 of Article 5 of New York's Civil Rights Law provide a cause of action for invasion of privacy when the plaintiff's "name, portrait or picture" is used for "advertising purposes, or for the purposes of trade," without the plaintiff's consent. Warren Spahn, one of the greatest left-handed pitchers of all time (of "Spahn and Sain and pray for rain" fame), brought an action against the defendant, the publisher of an unauthorized fictional biography of Spahn designed for juveniles, to enjoin publication and for compensatory damages for the invasion of privacy.

The trial court found that the "breadth and depth of the offending characteristics of the book are so all-pervasive as to render impracticable their complete recitation." The court then outlined the "offending characteristics." It noted first that the whole tenor of the book projected a false intimacy with Spahn. Dialogue was invented. Events were fabricated. For example, two chapters of the book dealt with Spahn's experiences in World War II. The book erroneously decorated Spahn with a Bronze Star for heroic acts that Spahn did not perform. Similarly, chapters dealing with Spahn's boyhood and teenage years inaccurately portray the relationship between Spahn and his father. The book romanticized the relationship, referring to "daily baseball sessions with his father," which never took place. With respect to Spahn's courtship, marriage, and family life, events and dialogue were entirely made up. The same is true of Spahn's baseball career. Throughout the book, events were taken out of context.]

· · · · · · · ·

While the essence of the right of privacy eludes precise verbal definition, it comprehends, in its pure form, the individual's absolute dominion and control over his "inviolate personality"—the individual's property right in his very being, whether manifested by his actions, his thoughts, his character, his appearance, his name. Dean Prosser, a leading authority in the law of torts, defines the law of privacy as comprising "four distinct kinds of invasion of four different interests. . . . 1. Intrusion upon the plaintiff's seclusion or solitude, or into his private affairs. 2. Public disclosure of embarrassing private facts about the plaintiff. 3. Publicity which places the plaintiff in a false light in the public eye. 4. Appropriation, for the defendant's advantage, of the plaintiff's name or likeness." (Prosser, "Privacy," 48 Cal. L. Rev. 383, 389).

· · · · · · · ·

During its early formative years, the right of privacy was shaped to meet the protection needed against the excesses of "yellow journalism" and the unauthorized practices of advertising, then in their embryonic stages. Today, the right must be construed in the context of a society that cannot cavalierly dismiss the pragmatic realities of our day. Scientific advances have multiplied the potential for infringement of the individual's sanctity, and the demands of our highly complex industrialized society dangerously engulf and threaten the perimeter of man's ever-shrinking sphere of personal liberty.

· · · · · · · ·

While untrue statements do not necessarily transform a book into the category of fiction, the all-pervasive distortions, inaccuracies, invented dialogue, and the narration of happenings out of context, clearly indicate, at the very least, a careless disregard for the responsibility of the press and within the context of this action, an abuse of the public's limited privilege to inquire into an individual's life.

· · · · · · · ·

Although so tightly interwoven as to defy extrication of the one from the other, the offending characteristics of the book comprehend a non-factual novelization of plaintiff's alleged life story and an unauthorized intrusion into the private realms of the baseball pitcher's life—all to Spahn's humiliation and mental anguish.

The subject purported biography transgresses the bounds of legitimate public interest by its breadth of reportorial coverage of those areas of plaintiff's life which defy classification as public, i.e., his deeply personal relationships with members of his immediate family and his introspective thoughts. Quantitatively, these trespasses upon plaintiff's private life represent a substantial portion of the book now under scrutiny. Qualitatively, the colorful portrayal of the intimate facets of Mr. Spahn's relationship with his father and his wife and the revelations of his innermost thinking . . . in many instances places the reader in the uncomfortable position of an embarrassed interloper upon another's private and personal domain.

Compounding the effect of these unlawful intrusions, plaintiff's uncontroverted testimony and evidence establish that factual errors so pervade and permeate these areas as well as the entire book as to render the whole story an "embroidered" and "embellished" version of Mr. Spahn's life. [Citation omitted.]

· · · · · · · ·

In effect then, the defendants have used Spahn's name and pictures to enhance the marketability and financial success of the subject book of which approximately 16,000 copies were sold at the retail price of $3.25 per copy. [Citation omitted.]

To return to the four category definition of "Privacy" by Dean Prosser, defendants have (1) intruded upon the plaintiff's solitude and into his private affairs, (2) disclosed embarrassing "facts" about the plaintiff, (3) placed the plaintiff in a false light in the public eye, and (4) appropriated, for defendants' advantage, the plaintiff's name and likeness. Such intrusion, disclosure and appropriation for commercial exploitation are proscribed by . . . the Civil Rights Law.

Accordingly, plaintiff is entitled to the relief sought; to wit, injunctive relief preventing the further publication and distribution of the WARREN SPAHN STORY in all its aspects and phases and is entitled to damages against both defendants in the sum of Ten Thousand Dollars ($10,000) and costs.

[The decision of the trial court in *Spahn* was affirmed by New York's intermediate appellate court (23 A.D.2d 216, 260 N.Y.S.2d 451 (1965)). This decision in turn was affirmed, without opinion, by New York's highest court (18 N.Y.2d 324, 274 N.Y.S.2d 877, 221 N.E.2d 543 (1966)). The Supreme Court of the United States vacated the judgment and remanded the case for further consideration in light of *Time, Inc. v. Hill* (387 U.S. 239 (1967)). On remand, the New York Court of Appeals affirmed, pointing out that the record supported a finding of "malice," as required by *Time, Inc. v. Hill*. Mercifully, the case was closed when the Supreme Court of the United States dismissed the subsequent appeal (393 U.S. 1046, 21 L.Ed.2d 600, 89 S.Ct. 676 (1969)).]

Namath v. Sports Illustrated
48 A.D.2d 487, 371 N.Y.S.2d 10 (1975)

[In one of the most memorable games in the history of professional football, Joe Namath led the upstart Jets to an upset victory over the Baltimore Colts in the 1969 Super Bowl, played in Miami on January 12. Namath's performance was highlighted with photographs in the January 20, 1969, issue of *Sports Illustrated* magazine. The magazine subsequently used one of the action photos of Namath in many of its advertisements to promote the sale of new subscriptions. In *Cosmopolitan* magazine, the photo was accompanied by the heading, "The Man You Love Loves Joe Namath." In *Life* magazine, the photo was accompanied by the heading, "How to Get Close to Joe Namath."

Namath claimed that *Sports Illustrated* violated his right of privacy under New York's Civil Rights Law, the same law Spahn relied on in the previous case. The defendant's motion to dismiss was granted at the trial court level. The court here affirms that dismissal.]

Before KUPFERMAN, J. P., and MURPHY, CAPOZZOLI, LAND and NUNEZ, JJ.

CAPOZZOLI, Justice:

Plaintiff sought substantial compensatory and punitive damages by reason of defendants' publication and use of plaintiff's photograph without his consent. That photograph, which was originally used by defendants, without objection from plaintiff, in conjunction with a news article published by them on the 1969 Super Bowl Game, was used in advertisements promoting subscriptions to their magazine, *Sports Illustrated*.

The use of plaintiff's photograph was merely incidental advertising of defendants' magazine in which plaintiff had earlier been properly and fairly depicted and, hence, it was not violative of the Civil Rights Law. [Citations omitted.]

Certainly, defendants' subsequent republication of plaintiff's picture was "in motivation, sheer advertising and solicitation. This alone is not determinative of the question so long as the law accords an exempt status to incidental advertising of the news medium itself." [Citations omitted.] Again, it was stated, at 15 A.D.2d p. 350, 223 N.Y.S.2d p. 744 of the cited case, as follows: "Consequently, it suffices here that so long as the reproduction was used to illustrate the quality and content of the periodical in which it originally appeared, the statute was not violated, albeit the reproduction appeared in other media for purposes of advertising the periodical."

Contrary to the dissent, we deem the cited case to be dispositive hereof. The language from the Namath advertisements relied upon in the dissent, does not indicate plaintiff's endorsement of the magazine *Sports Illustrated*. Had that been the situation, a completely different issue would have been presented. Rather, the language merely indicates, to the readers of those advertisements, the general nature of the contents of what is likely to be included in future issues of the magazine.

· · · · · · · ·

KUPFERMAN, Justice (dissenting).

It is undisputed that one Joseph W. Namath is an outstanding sports figure, redoubtable on the football field. Among other things, as the star quarterback of the New York Jets, he led his team to victory on January 12, 1969 in the Super Bowl in Miami.

This feat and the story of the game and its star were heralded with illustrative photographs in the January 20, 1969 issue of *Sports Illustrated*, conceded to be an outstanding magazine published by Time Incorporated and devoted, as its name implies, to the activities for which it is famous. Of course, this was not the first nor the last time that *Sports Illustrated* featured Mr. Namath and properly so.

The legal problem involves the use of one of his action photos from the January 20, 1969 issue in subsequent advertisements in other magazines as promotional material for the sale of subscriptions to *Sports Illustrated*.

Plaintiff contends that the use was commercial in violation of his right of privacy under §§ 50 and 51 of the Civil Rights Law. [Citation omitted.] Further, that because he was in the business of endorsing products and selling the use of his name and likeness, it interfered with his right to such sale, sometimes known as the right of publicity. [Citation omitted.] Defendants contend there is an attempt to invade their constitutional rights under the First and Fourteenth Amendments by the maintenance of this action and that, in any event, the advertisements were meant to show "the nature, quality and content" of the magazine and not to trade on the plaintiff's name and likeness.

Initially, we are met with the determination in a similar case, *Booth v. Curtis Publishing Co.*, 15 A.D.2d 343, 223 N.Y.S.2d 737 (1st Dept.) *aff'd without op.*, 11 N.Y.2d 907, 228 N.Y.S.2d 468, 182 N.E.2d 812 (1962) relied on by Baer, J., in his opinion at Special Term dismissing the complaint.

The plaintiff was Shirley Booth, the well-known actress, photographed at a resort in the West Indies, up to her neck in the water and wearing an interesting chapeau, which photo appeared in *Holiday* Magazine along with photographs of other prominent guests. This photo was then used as a substantial part of an advertisement for *Holiday*.

Mr. Justice Breitel (now Chief Judge Breitel) wrote: "Consequently, it suffices here that so long as the reproduction was used to illustrate the quality and content of the periodical in which it originally appeared, the statute was not violated, albeit the reproduction appeared in other media for purposes of advertising the periodical." 15 A.D.2d at p. 350, 223 N.Y.S.2d at p. 744.

However, this situation is one of degree. A comparison of the Booth and Namath photographs and advertising copy shows that in the Booth case, her name is in exceedingly small print, and it is the type of photograph itself which attracted attention. In the Namath advertisement, we find, in addition to the outstanding photograph, in *Cosmopolitan* Magazine (for women) the heading "The Man You Love Loves Joe Namath." There seems to be trading on the name of the personality involved in the defendants' advertisements.

This distinction between actual advertising use and use to inform, cf. *Bigelow v. Virginia*, 421 U.S. 809, 95 S.Ct. 2222, 44 L.Ed.2d 600 (1975) means that cases like *Time, Inc., v. Hill*, 385 U.S. 374, 87 S.Ct. 534, 17

L.Ed.2d 456 (1967) and *Cantrell v. Forest City Publishing Co.*, 419 U.S. 245, 95 S.Ct. 465 (1974) involving so-called "false light" portrayal are of only incidental interest. It is also a distinction accepted by Mr. Justice Breitel in that he recognized a right "to have one's personality, even if newsworthy, free from commercial exploitation at the hands of another . . . " *Booth v. Curtis Publishing Co., supra*, 15 A.D.2d at p. 351, 223 N.Y.S.2d at p. 745.

The complaint should not have been dismissed as a matter of law.

[Namath was affirmed again, this time with no written opinion, by New York's highest court at 39 N.Y.2d 897, 352 N.E.2d 584 (1976).]

A CASE STUDY—*VIRGIL v. TIME, INC.*
527 F.2d 1122 (9th Cir. 1975)

The causes of action arise out of a *Sports Illustrated* article entitled "The Closest Thing to Being Born." The article is about body surfing at the "Wedge," a public beach near Newport Beach, California, renown for its dangerousness. The article, written by *Sports Illustrated* staff writer Thomas Curry Kilpatrick, focuses on the body surfers at the Wedge. The plaintiff, Mike Virgil, a well-known body surfer at the Wedge, has the reputation of being the most daring of them all. Virgil was interviewed a number of times by Kilpatrick, and the article featured information from these interviews, along with photos of Virgil. In relevant part, the article provided: "He is somewhat of a mystery to most of the regular personnel, partly because he is quiet and withdrawn, usually absent from their get-togethers, and partly because he is considered to be somewhat abnormal." "Virgil's carefree style at the Wedge appears to have emanated from some escapades in his younger days, such as the time at a party when a young lady approached him and asked where she might find an ashtray. 'Why, my dear, right here,' said Virgil, taking her lighted cigarette and extinguishing it in his mouth. He also won a small bet one time by burning a hole in a dollar bill that was resting on the back of his hand. In the process he also burned two holes in his wrist."

Prior to publication, the article was reviewed by a *Sports Illustrated* "checker," who called Virgil to verify certain information. Virgil indicated he no longer wanted to be mentioned in the article. Virgil did not dispute the truth of the article. He told the checker he thought the article was going to be about his ability as a body surfer and that he did not know that the article would contain references to incidents not directly related to his body surfing. *Sports Illustrated* published the article over Virgil's objections.

Discussion

Arguably, a number of different causes of action arise out of the publication of the article. As is often the case with articles such as this, the practitioner's role is to sort through the various causes of action and identify and pursue the most viable.

The defamation cause of action. It should be noted at the outset that the article presents no substantial defamation claim. Remember, the gist of a defamation claim is a *false* statement injurious to reputation. Virgil acknowledges the truth of the matters contained in the Kilpatrick piece. True accounts are not the basis for defamation counts. At trial, Virgil expressly acknowledged that his cause of action was not for defamation.

Intrusion and misappropriation. Similarly, in the absence of a showing that Kilpatrick intruded into private areas in gathering information about Virgil, no intrusion cause of action is stated. The gist of the intrusion cause of action is an invasion of a right to solitude by the defendant in a manner which would be objectionable to a person of ordinary sensibilities. Normally, intrusion takes the form of peeking through windows, eavesdropping, excessive surveillance, or constant annoyance. The facts do not reveal an intrusion by Kilpatrick. Both the district court and the Ninth Circuit agreed that it was clear that Kilpatrick did not intrude on Virgil's solitude, particularly because all the interviews were freely given.

Both courts also agreed that Virgil did not state a misappropriation cause of action. The gist of that action is a commercial taking. Virgil's name or likeness is not being used primarily for commercial benefit. It is not as though the defendant was marketing bathing suits with Virgil's imprimatur on them.

False light privacy. In view of Virgil's admission of the truth of the matters contained in the article, he could not easily argue that the article placed him in a "false light in the public eye." Nonetheless, the district court found that the false light theory was available, although Virgil expressly abandoned this theory on appeal. The district court rationale, however, needs to be explored. It would appear that even true accounts can, if taken out of context, place the plaintiff in a false light. Thus, it is not entirely inaccurate to say that, unlike defamation, statements giving rise to a false light claim may be true if the overall impression of the article inaccurately portrays the plaintiff's character.

Public disclosure of private facts. Both the district court and the court of appeals agreed that the real gist of plaintiff's claim was public disclosure of private facts. Restatement § 652D refers to the tort as "Publicity Given to Private Life" and defines it as follows: "One who gives publicity to a matter concerning the private life of another is subject to liability to the other for unreasonable invasion of his privacy if the matter publicized is of a kind which: (a) would be highly offensive to a reasonable person, and (b) is not of legitimate concern to the public." Clearly, *Sports Illustrated* "publicized" certain facts about the plaintiff. The issue, so far as Virgil's cause of action was concerned, was whether those facts concerned the "private life" of Virgil. Comment C of the Restatement § 652 states: "The rule stated in this Section applies only to publicity concerning the private, as distinguished from the public, life of the individual. There is no liability when the defendant merely gives further publicity to information about the plaintiff which is already public. . . . Likewise there is no liability for giving further publicity to what the plaintiff himself leaves open to the public eye." *Sports Illustrated* argued that Virgil's voluntary disclosure of facts to Kilpatrick meant that the facts were not "private." Both the district court and the court of appeals disagreed, in light of the fact that Virgil withdrew his consent prior to the publication. The court of appeals concluded that the voluntary nature of the interview did not in itself render the facts public.

Sports Illustrated contended that the first amendment protected all truthful accounts. The court of appeals rejected this contention. While acknowledging the existence of a broad privilege to report news, the court concluded that publication of private facts served no legitimate news purpose. The only remaining question was whether the facts about Virgil were properly characterized as "private," or whether they were properly of legitimate concern to the public.

To resolve this issue, the court of appeals turned to the Restatement § 652D and noted that, in the final analysis, what is properly of legitimate concern to the public turns on the mores of the community. This being the case, the district court was entirely correct in concluding that all triable issues of fact be presented to the jury, which is in the best position to determine community standards. Virgil was entitled to have a jury determine whether that portion of the article which exposed private facts about Virgil was legitimately newsworthy.

ADDITIONAL NOTES

1. *Cepeda v. Cowles Magazines and Broadcasting, Inc.*, 392 F.2d 417 (9th Cir. 1968), *cert. denied* 393 U.S. 840 (1968). The "Baby Bull" Orlando Cepeda was the plaintiff in a defamation lawsuit that took over 5 years to resolve. Cepeda found himself trapped in a legal "pickle," in which the rules of defamation changed from one inning to the next. Although *Look* magazine defamed Cepeda by saying he was "not a team man" and that he was "temperamental, uncooperative and underproductive,"

Cepeda was unable to show actual malice and eventually lost the suit. Interestingly, when Cepeda first brought the suit, he was under no obligation to prove actual malice.

2. *Dempsey v. Time Incorporated*, 43 Misc. 2d 754, 252 N.Y.S.2d 186 (1964). Heavyweight champion Jack Dempsey brought a defamation action in the wake of a *Sports Illustrated* article suggesting that Dempsey used "loaded gloves" when he beat Jess Willard for the heavyweight title in 1919. According to the report, Dempsey's gloves were loaded with plaster of paris. The court denied the defendant's motion to dismiss, saying Dempsey introduced sufficient evidence of actual malice.

3. The modern sports celebrity will probably be viewed as a public figure for defamation purposes in most cases. This is particularly true if the account relates to the athlete's performance, as was the case in *Cepeda* and *Dempsey*. But what if the defamatory material relates to an aspect of the performer's private life? For example, how would the courts view a report alleging that the athlete is a homosexual? Assuming the allegation is false, a good argument could be made that the plaintiff is a private figure for purposes of this litigation and need not prove actual malice, according to *Gertz*. And if the report is true, the plaintiff's claim would be for public disclosure of private facts, not defamation.

4. Intrusion cases are relatively rare, but it is easy to see how the tort might arise in sports. Owners of clubs, eager to protect their investment, might be moved to unusual lengths to check on the activities of their players. The tort might thus arise in the manner of an overzealous bed check. In the early 1960s, it was reported that the Yankees hired private investigators to follow players. One perhaps apocryphal account had the Yanks following Tony Kubek and Bobby Richardson. Kubek and Richardson had squeaky clean reputations, and, as the story goes, the Yankees wanted to see if they were "for real." The erstwhile keystone combination proved that their reputations were well deserved. The Yankees reportedly came up empty after repeatedly following the two into ice cream parlors and Disney-like movies.

Al Davis, the renegade owner of the Los Angeles (or is it Oakland?) Raiders has on occasion implied a willingness to closely monitor the activities of his players. In another context, an overzealous press seems quite capable of intruding on an athlete's solitude in the quest for new information.

5. Misappropriation cases are bountiful. A memorable one is the so-called Human Cannonball case, *Zacchini v. Scripps-Howard Broadcasting*, 433 U.S. 562 (1977). Hugo Zacchini perfected a human cannonball act. Without his consent, a television station videotaped and broadcast Zacchini's entire act. (The actual time elapsed from takeoff to landing was less than 15 seconds.) The Supreme Court found that Hugo stated a cause of action and had the right to control the viewing of his act.

Compare *Gautier v. Pro-Football, Inc.*, 278 A.C. 431, 106 N.Y.S.2d 553 (1951). Arsene Gautier, an animal trainer, performed his act at halftime of a football game. He sued when the act was televised without his permission. The New York court dismissed his claim.

The more common misappropriation case in sports arises when the defendant makes use of the athlete's name for a purely commercial purpose, without the athlete's consent. *Uhlaender v. Henricksen*, 316 F. Supp. 1277 (D. Minn. 1970), is illustrative. In *Uhlaender*, the Major League Baseball Players' Association successfully enjoined the manufacturer of a table game from using players' names without consent. The court held that the players had proprietary interests in their names, likenesses, and accomplishments, significant enough in degree to justify the injunctive relief. *Palmer v. Schonhorn Enterprises*, 96 N.J. Super 72, 232 A.2d 458 (1967), is very similar to *Uhlaender*. In *Palmer*, a group of golfers successfully enjoined the sale of a golf game. While the court recognized that a celebrity's right to privacy is somewhat limited, the use of a celebrity's name for a commercial purpose other than the dissemination of news or information is invasive.

Orlando Cepeda lost another tough one in *Cepeda v. Swift and Company*, 415 F.2d 1205 (8th Cir. 1969). In the nightcap of Cepeda's litigation doubleheader, the Baby Bull sued Swift, a meat company, for the unauthorized use of Orlando's name, likeness, photograph, and signature in an advertising campaign promoting the sale of hot dogs. Cepeda had an agreement with Wilson Sporting Goods Company by which Wilson had the exclusive right to commercially exploit the Cepeda name. Wilson struck an agreement with Swift by which Cepeda baseballs could be purchased with wrappers from Swift products. The court found that, in light of Cepeda's agreement with Wilson, he had no claim against Swift.

Uhlaender, *Palmer*, and *Cepeda II* are offered as examples of the legion of misappropriation cases. The basic, well-established principle is that sports figures do possess a limited "right of publicity"—a right to control the manner in which their personalities are commercially exploited.

6. The preoccupation of the modern press with the private lives of public figures creates fertile ground for public disclosure of private facts causes of action. This was especially evident at Wimbledon in 1984, where the players complained about the propensity of the English press to report about their private lives. It is not at all unreasonable to anticipate litigation in this area. The litigation, in turn, will help define the parameters of the tort, particularly if the scope of the "news" privilege is articulated with some degree of clarity.

7. It should be noted that the Supreme Court has not, as of this writing, clarified the false light privacy rules. In *Time, Inc. v. Hill*, 385 U.S. 374 (1967), the court ruled that the plaintiff in such a case had to show actual malice. In the wake of *Gertz*, the question is whether *Time, Inc.*

is still good law. If the defamation rules apply in the false light context, it would appear that *Gertz* modifies *Time, Inc.* in regard to the private-person plaintiff.

8. Doctors who reveal medical information about their athlete-patients might find themselves defending defamation or privacy suits. Weistart and Lowell address the problem as a form of medical malpractice at 989–990.

9. Even though an abundance of information relates to defamation generally, there is a paucity of information concerning specific sports cases and sports figures, which is surprising because of the number of defamation cases arising in sports.

One article, however, outlines the referees' defamation case. See Melvin Narol and Stuart Dedopolous, "Defamation: A Guide to Referees' Rights," 16 TRIAL 42 (1980). The authors, both of whom are attorneys and basketball officials, predict an increase in defamation litigation by referees. They attribute this to the unwillingness of sports officials to continue to be subjected to verbal abuses and the like.

Although the authors list several issues to be considered in the referees' defamation case, they concentrate on one. In their opinion, the key issue is whether the sports official will be considered a "public figure." Because of the exposure through television, radio, and print media, the authors would regard an NBA referee as being within the public figure category. On the other hand, they feel a professional boxing judge would not fall into that category because of limited media coverage of boxing.

Some factors to consider in evaluating whether the referee is a public official are the level of competition being officiated; the number of years the sports official has been officiating; whether the athletic contest was broadcast on radio or television; and the sports official's notoriety in the particular sports community. In light of these factors, the official will fall on a continuum between public figure and private individual. At the public figure end would be an NBA referee. Moving toward the middle, the authors place there the Amateur Athletic Union and semi-professional and other similarly situated officials. In the middle falls the college sports official. The high-school official would fall into the private individual classification. And clearly, volunteer officials in Little League and community center games would be private individuals for defamation purposes.

Authorities who cover defamation and privacy generally are listed in the following bibliography.

BIBLIOGRAPHY

"Accommodation of Reputational Interests and Free Press: A Call for a Strict Interpretation of Gertz," 11 FORDHAM LAW JOURNAL 401 (1982–83).

"Defamation and Invasion of Privacy Actions in Typical Employee Relations Situations," 13 LINCOLN LAW REVIEW 1 (1982).

"Defamation Law: Once a Public Figure Always a Public Figure?" 10 HOFSTRA LAW REVIEW 803 (1982).

"Public Figure Plaintiff v. the Nonmedia Defendant in Defamation Law: Balancing the Respective Interests," 68 IOWA LAW REVIEW 518 (1983).

Treece, J., "Commercial Exploitation of Names, Likenesses and Personal Histories," 51 TEXAS LAW REVIEW 637 (1973).

Yasser, Raymond, "Defamation as a Constitutional Tort: With Actual Malice for All," 12 TULSA LAW JOURNAL 601 (1977).

6

Worker's Compensation Laws
and the Athlete

This chapter addresses the general issue of whether athletes are "employees" as that term is used in most worker's compensation schemes. In regard to the professional athlete, the issue is not so difficult. It is easy to see, for example, that an athlete on a professional team is an employee of that team. A difficult issue is whether individual performers (tennis players, golfers, or jockeys) can properly be viewed as employees for worker's compensation purposes. The most vexing questions arise in the context of the scholarship athlete. Are scholarship athletes "employees" of the educational institution which provides them with the scholarship? Before delving into these problems, a brief general note about worker's compensation is in order.

Every American jurisdiction has enacted some form of a worker's compensation law. Generally, worker's compensation schemes make the employer strictly liable for an injury to an employee that occurs within the scope of employment. An employee within the protection of the act, in turn, agrees that the statutory remedy is the sole remedy against the employer and thus waives the right to pursue a common law action against the employer. The rationale for the imposition of strict liability is that the employer is in the best position to bear the costs connected with such injuries. The theory is that injuries to workers are properly absorbed as a cost of doing business—in the same manner as equipment losses are absorbed. Such losses are inherent in business and are appropriately viewed as a production cost to be passed on to consumers.

Worker's compensation statutes typically require that the employer secure insurance to cover the costs of such injuries. Insurance rates are often regulated by the state so that the burden is spread evenly over the entire industry. The failure to obtain insurance exposes the employer to both criminal sanctions and civil suits. In the latter, the employer is deprived of the common law defenses of contributory negligence and assumption of risk.

In most worker's compensation schemes, the injured employee's measure of damages is limited. Although the injured employee is usually entitled to receive full compensation for medical expenses, the other items of tort damages are statutorily constrained. Only a percentage of the average weekly wages for the period of the disability can be recovered. The amount of recovery for disfigurement is statutorily prescribed or determined by a worker's compensation board.

Worker's compensation schemes reflect a type of bargain between employers and employees. The terms of the bargain are that employees give up their rights to pursue common law claims (with the promise of full recovery but with the danger of no recovery) in exchange for a certain, but limited, recovery under the worker's compensation act. The employer, in turn, relinquishes common law defenses and in return enjoys the assurance that damage awards will be limited. In deference to this common sense bargain, most courts tend to liberally construe worker's compensation laws so as to bring as many cases as reasonably possible under the law.

The professional team sport athlete. It is fair to say that professional team sport athletes are considered to be employees of their team for worker's compensation purposes. In fact, most standard player contracts reflect this understanding in salary continuation clauses. The standard player contract in the National Basketball Association, for example, provides that "the Player shall be entitled to receive his full salary for the season in which the injury was sustained, less all workmen's compensation benefits . . . payable to the player by reason of said injury." It should be noted, however, that a few states specifically exclude professional athletes with salary continuation clauses from worker's compensation protection. By way of illustration, the Massachusetts Workmen's Compensation Law states that those "employed . . . in organized professional athletics" are not covered employees if their contracts provide that wages are to be paid during the period of the disability (Mass. Ann. Laws, ch. 152 § 1(14) (Michie/Law. Coop. 1976)). The obvious lesson here is that the practitioner must be familiar with the relevant worker's compensation scheme.

The individual performer. A separate issue arises when an individual performer has a contract with a promoter or a "backer." The individual performer who is out on his or her own is, quite obviously, no one's employee and thus would not be entitled to worker's compensation benefits. But the individual performer who has a relationship with a promoter might be an employee for worker's compensation purposes.

This issue has been litigated most frequently in cases dealing with injuries to jockeys. The jockey cases are useful by way of analogy in other contexts involving individual performers like golfers and tennis players. A representative jockey case is included in the material that follows.

The scholarship athlete. The athletic scholarship is fundamental to the modern American amateur sports milieu. The athlete's acceptance of the athletic scholarship creates a legal relationship between the athlete and the educational institution that grants the award. In a series of cases, scholarship athletes have sought to recover for their injuries under worker's compensation laws. The important issue in such litigation is whether scholarship athletes are employees of the educational institution which provides them with the scholarship. The cases and material that follow explain the legal implications of a finding that scholarship athletes are in fact employees for worker's compensation purposes. If scholarship athletes are employees, are they really amateurs? Is a system which depends so heavily on the athletic scholarship really an amateur sports system? And what are the other legal ramifications of coming to grips with the fact that our scholarship athletes are really not amateurs at all?

THE LANDMARK CASES

PROFESSIONAL ATHLETES

Metropolitan Casualty Insurance Company of New York v. Huhn
165 Ga. 667, 142 S.E. 121 (1928)

[Two minor league baseball players were killed in an automobile accident while traveling to a game. The widows sought compensation under Georgia's Workmen's Compensation Act. Georgia's Industrial Commission—the statutorily mandated worker's compensation board in Georgia—rendered an award to the widows. The employer and the insurance carrier appealed. The court affirmed the award.]

· · · · · · · ·

Plaintiffs in error contend that—

"There can be no recovery in this case, because the relation between the deceased baseball player and the Augusta Baseball Club is not that of employee and employer as referred to in the Georgia Workmen's Compensation Act, in that the evidence in this case does not show that at the time of the alleged injury the baseball player, for whose death this claim is made, was engaged in a 'productive industry' or in any industry as contemplated by the Georgia Workmen's Compensation Act, and especially as contemplated in the title of said act, since it appears without a doubt that this baseball player was under a contract with the Augusta Baseball Club to engage solely in a sport or pastime, and not in an industry, and therefore was not exposed to any hazard of any industry, and could not have met his death with any industrial accident."

It is true the baseball player for whose death the claim is made was not engaged in a "productive industry" at the time of the happening of the occurrence which resulted in his death; but he was engaged in "business operated for gain or profit." Section 2(a) of the Compensation Act is in part as follows: "Employees shall include any . . . individual, firm, association or corporation engaged in any business for gain or profit, except as hereinafter excepted." And section 2(b) in part is as follows: "Employee shall include every person, including a minor, in the service of another under any contract of hire or apprenticeship, written or implied," etc. In this case the baseball player who was killed was a person "in the service of another under any contract of hire," and therefore was an "employee" under section 2(b). . . .

Gross v. Pellicane
65 N.J. Super. 386, 167 A.2d 838 (1961)

[Jockeys are typically employed in one of two ways. One method of employment is as a "contract rider." The contract rider is bound to ride when the owner requests. More commonly, jockeys "free-lance." The free-lance rider contracts on a race-by-race basis. The usual practice is to permit contract riders to free-lance. Contract riders are appropriately viewed as employees for worker's compensation purposes. The more difficult issues arise in the context of the free-lance rider.

Gross was free-lancing at the time of his injury, although he was a contract rider for another owner. His free-lance agreement was with Mrs. Deming, a trainer, who in turn had an agreement with the owners, the Pellicanes. The Division of Workmen's Compensation concluded that Gross was an employee of Mrs. Deming and not an employee of the Pellicanes and made an award accordingly. The court affirmed.]

The respondent Lily Deming is a trainer licensed by the New Jersey Racing Commission. While she had trained horses for the Pellicanes for four or five years, it is uncontradicted that she operated a public training stable at Monmouth Park, training horses besides those belonging to the Pellicanes. The horse stalls were assigned to her by the track.

The oral agreement between Lily Deming and the Pellicanes was to the effect that she would train their horses for $10 per day per horse. The Pellicanes also paid veterinarian and blacksmith fees, but the ordinary training expenses, such as feed, the salaries of grooms and exercise boys, were absorbed by the trainer. Mrs. Deming hired extra help according to the number of horses she was training at the time.

The trainer had complete control over the racing of the Pellicane horses. She decided what races should be entered and what jockeys should be engaged. The owners could not discharge a jockey or take him off a particular horse. The Pellicanes could make suggestions concerning the entering of a particular race or the hiring of a particular jockey, but the final decision was up to the trainer.

This agreement between the trainer and the owners was renewable after every meet and turned out to be a continuing association. The Pellicanes would tell Mrs. Deming at the end of each track meet that they wanted her to go to the next track and take care of their horses there. Mrs. Pellicane testified that they could terminate their association with the trainer at the end of a meet if irreconcilable differences of opinion arose. However, she wasn't sure whether this could be done during a meet.

Mrs. Deming was authorized to withdraw moneys from the Pellicane account at the track. From this account she paid the jockey fees. If the funds on deposit were insufficient, she would pay the jockey fees from her own funds and obtain reimbursement from the Pellicanes. It is undisputed that the obligation for payment of the jockey fees was upon the owners. The track sent the owners a periodic statement of their account showing payment of jockey fees and to whom paid.

On the day prior to the race in question Mrs. Deming contacted the petitioner's agent and arranged for the petitioner to ride "Lady Glade" the next day. The trainer met the petitioner in the paddock approximately 10 to 20 minutes before the race and gave him his instructions as to the handling of the horse. The petitioner testified, "she told me that this horse had a lot of speed and to break this horse out of the gate if the horse could go right in front without me rushing her off her feet, but if she didn't show any speed in the first part to get everything in the last part." Gross also testified that Mrs. Deming could have taken him off the horse up to the time he was actually in the paddock, and if he didn't follow her instructions, she wouldn't engage him again. It was brought out on cross-examination that problems sometimes arose during the race and he would have to use his own judgment as to what to do.

• • • • • • • •

Two sections of the rules of the New Jersey State Racing Commission have been referred to by the parties herein. The first, Rule 340, requires all owners and/or trainers to carry compensation insurance for all their employees, including jockeys and apprentice jockeys. Rule 601 provides, "a licensed trainer may represent the owner in the matter of . . . the employment of jockeys."

The questions presented on this appeal are: 1) Whether the petitioner was an employee or an independent contractor, and if he was an employee, was the employment casual? 2) Who was the employer of the petitioner, the owners or the trainer of the horse?

N.J.S.A. 34:15–36 defines the terms "employer" and "employees" as used in the Workmen's Compensation Act as follows: " 'Employer' is declared to be synonymous with master, and includes natural persons, partnerships, and corporations; 'employee' is synonymous with servant, and includes all natural persons, including officers of corporations, who perform service for an employer for financial consideration."

The act is to be liberally construed to bring as many cases as possible within its coverage. [Citation omitted.]

It is well settled that basic to the existence of an employer-employee relationship is the employer's right to control the details on the employee's work, i.e., not what shall be done, but how it shall be done, and the right to discharge him. [Citations omitted.] If the person rendering the service is an independent contractor, these essentials are absent. [Citation omitted.] "The status of the petitioner is to be resolved upon the totality of the facts surrounding the relationship, with due regard for the attendant circumstances, the object in view, and the course of practice in its execution." [Citation omitted.]

The evidence in the instant case clearly shows that the petitioner was subject to the control of the trainer and was duty-bound by his contract to follow her instructions as to the manner in which the race should be run. The fact that the instructions given in the instant case may appear to be merely informative as to the speed and capabilities of the horse is of no consequence. It is the existence of the right to control and not the actual exercise of this right which is determinative. [Citation omitted.]

The fact that the petitioner would have to use his own judgment concerning unanticipated problems which arose during the race, and that he could not be discharged after the race commenced, does not belie the existence of the right to control and discharge, but is merely due to the practical exigencies of the industry in question. It is of no consequence that because of physical inability the trainer was unable to communicate his [sic] exercise of such authority to Gross.

Although there appears uncontradicted evidence of the existence of other criteria pointing to the conclusion that the petitioner was an independent contractor, nevertheless, said evidence is not sufficient to overcome the clear showing of the power of Mrs. Deming to control and discharge. [Citations omitted.]

Other jurisdictions have concluded that a free-lance jockey is an employee within the purview of Workmen's Compensation Acts. *Pierce v. Bowen*, 247 N.Y. 305, 160 N.E. 379 (Ct. App. 1928); *Drillon v. Industrial Accident Comm.*, 17 Cal.2d 346, 110 P.2d 64 (Sup. Ct. 1941); *Isenberg v. California Employment Stabilization Comm.*, 30 Cal.2d 34, 180 P.2d 11 (Sup. Ct. 1947).

The respondents rely upon *Whalen v. Harrison*, 51 F. Supp. 515 (D.C.N.D. Ill. 1943), which held that under facts similar to the instant case, "free-lance jockeys" were independent contractors and the owner of horses was not liable for social security taxes upon compensation paid by him to certain "free-lance jockeys" who rode for him. Judge Sullivan in that case concluded that such jockeys were not subject to any control taking a different view of the surrounding facts. However, without exploring this case further, suffice it to say that that decision concerned the Federal Social Security Act, 42 U.S.C.A. § 1107, and the instant case involves an application of our Workmen's Compensation Act.

Judge Sullivan, in the *Whalen* case, quoted with approval from *Ridge Country Club v. United States*, 135 F.2d 718, 721 (7 Cir. 1943), as follows: "We, too, look to the purpose of the statute and the intent of the legislature in enacting it, as well as the words used to carry out this intention. *Only certain classes are the beneficiaries of this social legislation, consisting chiefly of the ordinary wage earners*." (Emphasis supplied.)

Our Workmen's Compensation Act does not limit the term "employee" to narrow common-law concepts or ordinary wage earners, because it also "includes all natural persons . . . who perform service for an employer for financial consideration." [Citations omitted.]

The respondents contend that the employment was casual, citing *Moore v. Clarke*, 171 Md. 39, 187 A. 887, 107 A.L.R. 924 (Ct. App. 1936), and *East v. Skelly*, 207 Md. 537, 114 A.2d 822 (Ct. App. 1955) (both cases involving "free-lance jockeys"). The Maryland Compensation Act provides that it "shall not apply . . . to casual employees. . . . " Md. Annotated Code, Art. 101, sec. 68, subsec. 3. The Maryland act does not define the term "casual employees," as does our act. The Maryland Court of Appeals has construed an employment to be casual, where, though part of the employer's business, it was unconnected with past and future employment and contractual relations ceased when the employment was finished. *Moore v. Clarke, supra.*

Such is not the law of New Jersey because our Legislature has seen fit to define the casual employments which are excluded from the coverage of the act.

N.J.S.A. 34:15–36 provides: " . . . casual employments, which shall be defined, if in connection with the employer's business, as employment the occasion for which arises by chance or is purely accidental; or if not in connection with any business of the employer, as employment not regular, periodic or recurring" . . .

It is evident, and both the Pellicanes and Mrs. Deming readily admitted, that horse racing is a business. The question remains whether the occasion for the petitioner's employment arose by chance or is purely accidental. To state the question answers it. The employment of a jockey is an integral part of the business of racing horses, the occasion for which does not arise by chance or accident. Cf. *Graham v. Green*, 31 N.J. 207, 156 A.2d 241 (1959). [Citation omitted.]

The issue remains as to who was the petitioner's employer. It is the conclusion of this court that the respondent Mrs. Deming alone is responsible for the award in favor of Gross. The evidence clearly shows that Gross was hired and rode the horse in question as a result of an arrangement made between Mrs. Deming and the petitioner's agent. The trainer had complete control over the employment of a jockey and the manner in which he rode the horse. She alone had the right to discharge the jockey.

The Pellicanes were merely interested in results—that their horse was properly cared for and that he won as many horse races as possible. There was no contractual relationship between Gross and the Pellicanes. Mrs. Deming was an independent contractor who was uncontrolled by the Pellicanes in the training and racing of their horses. She was engaged in the business of training horses and she maintained a public stable. Mrs. Deming employed the jockeys in connection with her business as a trainer and not as an agent for the Pellicanes. Such was the understanding of all the parties and seems to be the custom of the racing industry.

The fact that the ultimate source of payment for the jockey fees was the Pellicanes does not prevent the aforesaid conclusion that Mrs. Deming was the employer of the petitioner. It is true that a prerequisite to the existence of an employment status is that there be a financial consideration flowing between the employer and the employee. [Citation omitted.] However, this requirement was satisfied in the case at bar. Mrs. Deming always made the payment of the jockey fees to the track whether from the owner's account or from her own funds and later obtained reimbursement from the owners. There was a financial consideration which flowed from Mrs. Deming to the petitioner.

It is the conclusion of this court that the petitioner Gross was an employee and not an independent contractor. The employment was not casual. The respondent Lily Deming was the sole employer of the petitioner. The petition against the respondent Pellicanes should be dismissed.

The award of the Division of Workmen's Compensation is affirmed.

AMATEUR ATHLETES

Van Horn v. Industrial Accident Commission
219 Cal. App. 2d 457, 33 Cal. Rptr. 169 (1963)

[Edward Van Horn was a star athlete in high school. The football coach of California State Polytechnic College (Cal Poly) recruited Van Horn to play football and promised him a job on campus. Van Horn enrolled at Cal Poly in September 1956 and played football during the fall term. He lived on campus and worked in the college cafeteria. In the summer of 1957, he got married and decided not to play football. In the spring of 1958, he returned to the team for spring practice, after the coach promised him that "he would receive assistance from the college of $50.00 at the beginning of each school semester and $75.00 rent money during the football playing season." Van Horn told his father that he decided to return to play football because he had been offered "a pretty good deal . . . to support his family." Thereafter, he received his checks in a timely fashion. The $50 checks contained the notation: "Scholarship." The $75 payments had no such notation and came from the coach's discretionary fund. Van Horn continued to play football through the 1958, 1959, and 1960 seasons and received his checks regularly. In October of 1960, he was killed in an airplane crash while returning from a game.

Following Van Horn's death, his widow and minor children applied for death benefits under California's Workmen's Compensation Act. The Industrial Accident Commission denied the application, concluding that Van Horn was not an employee rendering services within the meaning of the act. The District Court of Appeals reversed the commission, concluding that the commission's findings were not supported by the evidence.]

"The question of whether a worker is an employee within the meaning of the Compensation Act . . . is referred to as a question of mixed law and fact to be proved like any other question. [Citations omitted.] It is a question of fact upon which the judgment of the commission is conclusive where the facts are in dispute. It becomes a question of law only when but one inference can reasonably be drawn from the facts. Where two opposing inferences may be drawn from the evidence, and the inference accepted by the commission is reasonable, and is supported by evidence in the record, that inference must be sustained." [Citation omitted.]

" 'Employee' means every person in the service of an employer under any appointment or contract of hire or apprenticeship, express or implied, oral or written, whether lawfully or unlawfully employed . . .' "

[Citation omitted.] The state and all state agencies are employers subject to Workmen's Compensation liability. [Citation omitted.]

If services are voluntarily rendered without compensation, there is no employment relationship. [Citations omitted.] However, direct compensation in the form of wages is not necessary to establish the relationship so long as the service is not gratuitous. [Citations omitted.]

"Any person rendering service for another, other than as an independent contractor, or unless expressly excluded herein, is presumed to be an employee." [Citation omitted.] This presumption, together with evidence of a contract of employment or hire, casts upon the alleged employer the burden of overcoming the presumption. [Citation omitted.]

After a careful review of the evidence, we are of the opinion that the finding of the commission that there was no contract of employment is not supported by the evidence. The record reveals that petitioners established a prima facie case for benefits upon the presentation of evidence showing the alleged contract of employment. The coach, with whom it was shown that decedent made the alleged contract, testified at length; yet nowhere in his testimony is there a denial by him that he made a contract with decedent.

· · · · · · · ·

In view of the lack of contradictory testimony in the present record, we conclude that the finding of the commission is contrary to the evidence. The opinion of the commission indicates that in support of this finding it relied on a written statement made by decedent in which he stated that he would like to play football at the college and planned to finance his way through school on a scholarship. From this statement the commission drew the inference that decedent did not consider himself to be an employee. The commission identifies this document as an application "for the scholarship." A reading of the record indicates that the document was an application prepared by the decedent for admission to the college in September 1956. Since the evidence submitted by petitioners was that the agreement between decedent and the coach was made after the football season of 1957, it is apparent that the document on which the commission relied has no probative value on the issue of whether the alleged contract was subsequently made and is insufficient to support any inference as to the relationship of the decedent to the college when he rejoined the team.

As we have stated, the commission concluded that by playing football for the college the decedent was not "rendering services" within the meaning of the Workmen's Compensation Act. While the case is one of first impression in this jurisdiction, there is authority for the proposition that one who participates for compensation as a member of an athletic team may be an employee within the statutory scheme of the Workmen's Compensation Act. (*Metropolitan Casualty Ins. Co. of New York v. Huhn*, 165 Ga. 667; 142 S.E. 121, 59 A.L.R. [professional baseball player]; *University of Denver v. Nemeth*, 127 Colo. 385, 257 P.2d 423 [state college football player].) The fact that academic credit is given for participation in the activity is immaterial. It has been held that one may have the dual capacity of student and employee in respect to an activity. [Citation omitted.] . . . The conclusion of the commission is erroneous and, as a determination of law, is not binding on an appellate tribunal. [Citations omitted.]

The commission also made the following finding: "The scholarship, when awarded, was for an entire year and was not dependent upon participating in sports. Even if the Deceased had not played in a single game, he still would have received the scholarship. Also, scholarships were awarded on scholastic records, rather than athletic prowess. The football coach was not consulted in passing on the applications." The record clearly contradicts these findings. The uncontradicted evidence was that to receive an athletic scholarship a student must have maintained a 2.2 grade average while carrying twelve units, must be a member of an athletic team, and be recommended by the coach to the scholarship committee. He recommended only those who were on the team. There was evidence that the coach had no power to overrule the committee or to terminate a scholarship before the term for which it was granted had elapsed but that evidence does not support the inference that there was no relationship between the "scholarship" and decedent's athletic prowess or participation. The only inference to be drawn from the evidence is that decedent received the "scholarship" because of his athletic prowess and participation. The form of remuneration is immaterial. A court will look through form to determine whether consideration has been paid for services. [Citations omitted.]

The opinion of the commission sets forth the proposition that to conclude that one who has an athletic scholarship is an employee entitled to workmen's compensation benefits would impose a heavy burden on institutions of learning, would discourage the granting of scholarships, and, therefore, would be against public policy. We find no authority to the effect that an award in the present instance would be against public policy. On the contrary, the public policy of the State is declared in the Workmen's Compensation Act. [Citation omitted.] All provisions of the workmen's compensation law should be liberally construed to effect the law's beneficent purposes. [Citation omitted.] The theory of the compensation act as to death cases is that the dependents of the employee killed through some hazard of his employment shall be compensated for the loss of the support they were receiving from him at the time of his death. [Citation omitted.] Where there is any reasonable doubt as to the jurisdiction, the courts must resolve such doubts in favor of jurisdiction of the commission. [Citation omitted.]

The Workmen's Compensation Act is, in effect, a socially-enforced bargain which compels an employee to give up his valuable right to sue in the courts for full recovery of damages under common-law theories in return for a certain, but limited, award. It compels the employer to give up his right to assert common-law defenses in return for assurance that the amount of recovery by the employee will be limited. In the evolution of workmen's compensation legislation and case law there has been an increasing recognition of its purpose to distribute the risk of service-connected injuries or death by charging all enterprises with the costs and not merely those enterprises which produce saleable products and which can therefore transfer the cost of injuries to the consumers of products. Thus, churches, charitable organizations, non-profit hospitals, universities and other large, publicly-supported institutions have been held to be employers within the meaning of the Workmen's Compensation Act. [Citations omitted.]

It cannot be said as a matter of law that every student who receives an "athletic scholarship" and plays on the school athletic team is an employee of the school. To so hold would be to thrust upon every student who so participates an employee status to which he has never consented and which would deprive him of the valuable right to sue for damages. Only where the evidence establishes a contract of employment is such inference reasonably to be drawn. *State Compensation Ins. Fund v. Industrial Com'n*, 135 Colo. 570, 314 P.2d 288, cited by respondents, is a case in which a member of a college football team received a scholarship for tuition. There the evidence did not establish a contract of hire to play football and thus did not support a finding of an employee-employer relationship.

The commission also made a finding that "the evidence is not clear as to the identity of the employer" and that "the alumni association which raised the money for the scholarship or the student body might just as well have been the employer, if not more logically so." The record reveals that the fifty-dollar checks received by the decedent were issued by the college, that the coach was a member of the college faculty in control of the athletic activities, and that the football team represented the college in intercollegiate games. There is no uncertainty in the record. The fact that the funds were contributed by the Mustang Booster Club is not determinative of who is the employer. [Citations omitted.]

For the reasons set forth above, the order of the commission is annulled. The matter is remanded to the commission for further proceedings consistent herewith.

Hearing denied: SCHAUER and McCOMB, JJ., dissenting.

The Matrix of Landmark Cases

In addition to *Van Horn*, two Colorado cases bear heavily on the question of whether scholarship athletes are employees for worker's compensation purposes—*University of Denver v. Nemeth*, 127 Colo. 385, 257 P.2d 423 (1953) and *State Compensation Insurance Fund v. Industrial Commission* (Dennison), 135 Colo. 570, 314 P.2d 288 (1957).

Nemeth

Nemeth was a regularly enrolled student in the College of Business Administration at the University of Denver during the 1949–1950 academic year. He was also a football player. Although he did not have a "scholarship," he received $50 per month from the university for cleaning the campus tennis courts. In lieu of payment for housing, Nemeth took care of the dormitory furnace and cleaned the sidewalks near the dorm. In the spring of 1950, Nemeth suffered a back injury during spring football practice.

Nemeth went before the Industrial Commission, claiming that he was employed to play football at the university and that his injury arose out of that employment. He was successful before the Industrial Commission. On appeal, the district court affirmed the commission. The Colorado Supreme Court affirmed and held that Nemeth was an employee who was injured in the course of his employment and was thus entitled to worker's compensation benefits.

The Supreme Court noted that the evidence revealed that Nemeth's jobs depended on his football performance:

It appears from the record that Nemeth was informed by those having authority at the University, that "it would be decided on the football field who receives . . . the jobs." He participated in football practice, and after a couple of weeks a list of names was read which included Nemeth's name, and he was then given . . . a job. One witness said: "If you worked hard (in football) you got a meal ticket." Another testified that, the man who produced in football would get . . . a job. The football coach testified that . . . the job ceased when the student was "cut from the squad."

The court went on to observe that: "It has been repeatedly held in this state, and in every other jurisdiction, that the Workmen's Compensation Act must be liberally construed to give effect to its purposes." The court thus concluded that Nemeth was in fact an employee whose injury arose out of the employment. An injury arises out of the employment if it arises out of the nature, conditions, obligations, or incidents of the employment, in other words, out of the employment looked at in any of its aspects. It should be noted that *Nemeth* is not a typical case since the athlete was not a scholarship recipient. But *Nemeth* is important because it indicates judicial willingness to look at the real nature of the relationship between a student athlete and the university or college for which he plays. If the athlete is in fact being compensated *because* of his athletic performance, he is perhaps most accurately viewed as an employee for worker's compensation purposes. This kind of quid pro quo arrangement is the earmark of an employee-employer relationship.

Dennison

A scant four years later, the Colorado Supreme Court confronted the issue again. Billy Dwade Dennison was employed at a filling station when the football coach at Fort Lewis A & M College asked if he would be interested in playing football. Dennison was unwilling to give up the income from the filling station job, and a deal was negotiated with the university. Dennison was employed by the college to manage the student lounge and to work on the college farm. He was paid the regular student rate for this work. Dennison also received an athletic scholarship which operated as a tuition waiver. Dennison's work schedule was arranged to accommodate his football-related activities. In September 1955, Dennison received a fatal head injury.

Dennison's widow was awarded death benefits by the Industrial Commission, and that award was affirmed by the district court. In a curious and poorly reasoned one and a half page opinion, the Colorado Supreme Court reversed the judgment and remanded to the district court with directions to enter an order dismissing the claim. The court distinguished *Nemeth*: "the distinction is at once apparent. In [*Nemeth*] claimant's employment as a student worker depended wholly on his playing football, and it is clear that if he failed to perform as a football player he would lose the job provided for him by the university." Dennison, on the other hand, did not, in the court's view, receive his benefits in consideration of athletic participation: "[N]one of the benefits he received could, in any way, be claimed as consideration to play football, and there is nothing in the evidence that is indicative of the fact that the contract of hire by the college was dependent upon his playing football, that such employment would have been changed had deceased not engaged in the football activities."

This is judicial disingenuousness at best. Surely it is accurate to say that Dennison, like Nemeth, received the university benefits in exchange for participation in football. The cases cannot be meaningfully distinguished.

A CASE STUDY—*RENSING v. INDIANA STATE UNIVERSITY BOARD OF TRUSTEES*
437 N.E.2d 78 (Ind. Ct. App. 1982), *rev'd,* 444 N.E.2d 1170 (Ind. 1983)

On February 4, 1974, Indiana State University offered Fred Rensing a football scholarship. The terms of the scholarship were contained in a "financial aid agreement" and a "tender of financial assistance." In relevant part, the financial aid agreement provided:

This is to certify that Indiana State University will award you an educational grant if you meet the academic requirements of Indiana State University and the National Collegiate Athletic Association.

Your grant will consist of the following: Tuition Fees; Room and Board; and Book Allowance for a period of One Year.

This award may be renewed each year for a total of four years as long as you are academically qualified and abide by acceptable conduct standards.
In the event that you incur an injury, during supervised conduct of your sport, of such severity that the doctor-director of your student health service deems it inadvisable for you to continue to participate, this grant will be continued for as long as you are otherwise eligible for competition. In this instance, Indiana State University will ask you to assist in the conduct of the athletic program within the limits of your physical capabilities.

The tender of financial assistance provided in relevant part:

The award is made in accordance with the rules of this institution and the applicable provisions of the Constitution and Bylaws of the National Collegiate Athletic Association (NCAA). Your acceptance means that you also accept these provisions and agree to abide by them.

The benefits of the award are effective August 1974 to May 1975.

A summary of the applicable rules of the NCAA are set forth on the reverse side of this form. Please read carefully.

1. In accepting this Tender of Financial Assistance, the recipient certifies: (a) He is aware that any employment earnings during term time and any other financial assistance from any source other than that provided for in this award must be reported immediately to the director of Athletics of the institution making the award. (b) The aid provided in the Tender will be canceled if the recipient signs a professional sports contract or accepts money for playing in an athletic contest.

2. Financial aid may be awarded for any term or session during which the student-athlete is in attendance as a regularly enrolled undergraduate. The re-

newal of a scholarship or grant-in-aid award shall be made on or before July 1 prior to the academic year it is to be effective.

3. Maximum permissible financial aid may not exceed "commonly accepted educational expenses"; i.e., tuition and fees, room and board, required course related supplies and books.

4. A student-athlete may not receive financial assistance other than that "administered by" the institution except that financial assistance may be received from anyone upon whom the student-athlete is naturally or legally dependent. . . .

5. When unearned financial aid is awarded to a student and athletic ability is taken into consideration in making the award, such aid combined with other aid the student-athlete may receive from employment during semester or term time, other scholarships and grants-in-aid (including governmental grants for educational purposes) and like sources, may not exceed commonly accepted educational expenses as defined in Paragraph 3 above . . .

Institutional aid MAY NOT BE GRADATED OR TERMINATED during the period of its award:

1. Because of the recipient's athletic ability or his contribution to a team's success.

2. Because an injury prevents the recipient from participating in athletics.

Institutional aid MAY BE GRADATED OR TERMINATED during the period of its award if the recipient:

1. Does not satisfy the stated institutional academic requirements for like scholarships or grants-in-aid.

2. Voluntarily renders himself ineligible for intercollegiate athletic competition.

3. Fraudulently misrepresents any information on his application, letter of intent or tender.

4. Engages in serious misconduct warranting substantial disciplinary penalty by the appropriate institutional committee or agency.

Such GRADATION OR TERMINATION of an award may occur if:

The action is taken by the institution's regular disciplinary and/or awards authority.

The student-athlete has had opportunity for a hearing.

The action is based on institutional policy applicable to the general student body.

Rensing accepted the offer and "signed" on April 29, 1974. At the end of Rensing's first academic year, Rensing's scholarship was renewed for the 1975–1976 year under substantially the same conditions.

On April 24, 1976, Rensing was rendered a quadriplegic as a result of an injury during spring football practice.

On August 22, 1977, Rensing filed a claim under Indiana Workmen's Compensation Act seeking recovery for permanent total disability and for medical and hospital expenses incurred as a result of the injury. After a hearing in February of 1979, the Industrial Board's Hearing Member issued his findings and award:

. . . That on the 24th day of April, 1976, the Plaintiff herein sustained personal injury by reason of an accident arising out of and in the course of his participating as a football player for the Defendant in a Spring football practice scrimmage; that Plaintiff's said accidental injury consisted of a fracture dislocation of the cervical spine at the 4–5 vertebrae, resulting in a permanent total disability to Plaintiff's body as a whole.

It is further found that on April 24, 1976 at the time of Plaintiff's said accidental injury, Plaintiff was not in the employ of the Defendant herein; that the relationship of employer-employee within the meaning of the Indiana Workmen's Compensation Act [IC 22–3–1–1 et seq.] is contractual in character; that the relationship of the employer-employee always arises out of a contract, either express or implied; that one seeking recovery under the Act must bring themselves [sic] within its terms; that recovery of compensation depends upon the existence of the relation of the employer and employee; that the burden of proving by competent evidence of probative value the various essential elements of the Plaintiff's case before the Industrial Board of Indiana, including the establishment of the relationship of the employer and employee within the meaning of the Indiana Workmen's Compensation Act, rests solely upon the employee; that the Plaintiff failed to sustain his burden in establishing the necessary relationship of employer and employee within the meaning of the Indiana Workmen's Compensation Act.

It is further found that the undersigned Hearing Member has indulged in a measure of liberality in construing the legislative definition of "employee" however, the Plaintiff has failed to bring himself within the terms of one seeking recovery under the Indiana Workmen's Compensation Act.

AWARD

IT IS, THEREFORE, CONSIDERED, ORDERED AND ADJUDGED by the Industrial Board of Indiana that the Plaintiff shall take nothing . . . by his Form 9 Application for the Adjustment of Claim for Compensation, filed on the 22nd day of August, 1977.

Dated this 24th day of May, 1979.

Rensing, following the statutorily prescribed procedure, appealed first to the full Industrial Board, which affirmed in full the report of the Hearing Member. Rensing then appealed to the Indiana Court of Appeals, which reversed the Industrial Board in a 2 to 1 decision and remanded for a determination of benefits. The Court of Appeals majority decision reviewed both the relevant worker's compensation law principles and the matrix of relevant cases in reaching its conclusion.

The Court of Appeals began by noting that the parties agreed that "some manner of contract existed between them." The question was whether there was a "contract for hire or employment" within the meaning of the Workmen's Compensation Act. After noting that the proper scope of review compelled deference to the decision of the Industrial Board, the court nonetheless reversed the board, finding Rensing's evidence "so conclusive . . . as to lead to only one conclusion"—that Rensing was in fact an employee within the meaning of the act. In so concluding, the court pointed out that the beneficent purposes of the act supported a liberal construction: "In applying the statutory definition of employee . . . , a measure of liberality should be indulged . . . to the end that in doubtful cases an injured workman" is compensated.

The court's determination that the requisite employer-employee relationship existed rested on the definitions of "employer" and "employee" found in the act. An employer was defined to include "the state and any political division, . . . any individual, firm, association or corporation . . . using the services of another for pay." An employee was defined as "every person, including a minor, in the service of another, under any contract of hire or apprenticeship, written or implied, except one whose employment is both casual and not in the usual course of trade . . . of the employer."

Viewing the evidence, the court found that the conclusion was inescapable: the requisite relationship existed. Rensing and the university "bargained for an exchange in the manner of employer and employee of Rensing's football talents for certain scholarship benefits."

Rensing's employment was clearly more than "casual." The court noted its own definition of "casual work" as being work which is "not permanent nor periodically regular but occasional." It also noted that there was no "hard and fast rule . . . to draw the line between employments which are casual and those which are not." Each case had to be judged on its own merits. Rensing's employment, however, was obviously not casual, since it clearly was "periodically regular," even though not permanent: "The uncontradicted evidence revealed that for the team members football is a daily routine for 16 weeks each year. Additionally, during the 'off-season' the 'student-athlete' must daily work out to maintain his physical skills and attributes, thereby enhancing his eligibility for the team which is the basis for his scholarship."

Since Rensing's employment was not casual, it was not necessary to reach the question of whether the employment was "in the usual course of trade." Nonetheless, the court made it clear that if it were to decide that question it would find that "football competition must properly be viewed as an aspect of the university's overall occupation sufficient to bring it within the usual course of trade of the university." In this regard, the court stated: "It is manifest from the record . . . that maintaining a football team is an important aspect of the University's overall business or profession of educating students. . . . Suffice it to say, it was uncontroverted that football . . . and athletes . . . play a beneficial role . . . at the University . . . [and that] the University has prospered athletically through nationally recognized . . . teams."

Judge Young, dissenting, stated that he did not believe that student athletes are employees within the meaning of the Indiana Workmen's Compensation Act. He cited *Van Horn* as support for his belief. While agreeing that "a measure of liberality should be indulged," Judge Young was of the opinion that the legislature did not intend that student-athletes be treated as employees. Although Rensing indeed entered into a contract, it was not a "contract of hire."

Discussion

The Supreme Court of Indiana agreed with dissenting Judge Young, holding that no employer-employee relationship existed between the student and the university on the basis of Rensing's receipt of a scholarship and that Rensing was therefore not entitled to worker's compensation benefits. The court reinstated the decision of the Industrial Board.

The court first noted that since Rensing was appealing from a "negative judgment" of the Industrial Board, it would not disturb the findings unless the evidence "leads inescapably to a contrary result." Even though worker's compensation laws are to be "liberally construed," Rensing was properly denied benefits. The primary consideration was that Rensing and the university did not intend to enter into an employer-employee relationship:

It is clear that while a determination of the existence of an employee-employer relationship is a complex matter involving many factors, the primary consideration is that there was an intent that a contract of employment, either express or implied, did exist. In other words, there must be a mutual belief that an employer-employee relationship did exist. . . . It is evident from the documents which formed the agreement in this case that there was no intent to enter into an employee-employer relationship at the time the parties entered into the agreement.

As evidence of this lack of intent, the court pointed to the fact that the NCAA constitution and bylaws were incorporated by reference into Rensing's agreement. The constitution and bylaws in turn clearly articulated the policy that intercollegiate sports are to be viewed "as part of the educational system and are clearly distinguished from the professional sports business." Both Rensing and his parents signed the agreement—they therefore were deemed to have placed their imprimatur on the policy statement. They were deemed to have understood that Rensing was a student-athlete and not an employee. Rensing's benefits (tuition, room, board, fees, and book allowance) were not considered "pay" by anyone concerned. The university and the NCAA considered Rensing an eligible amateur. Rensing, in turn, did not consider the benefits as income since he did not report them for income tax purposes.

As further evidence of this lack of intent, the court noted that the Indiana General Assembly distinguished between awarding financial aid and hiring employees by specifically granting the power to grant aid to the Boards of Trustees of state institutions. Furthermore, it found that the Indiana statute which directed employers to make contributions to the unemployment fund for "all individuals attending . . . school . . . who, in lieu of remuneration for . . . services, receive . . . meals, lodging, books [or] tuition" was not intended to cover Rensing because "Rensing was not working at a regular job for the University." Scholarship recipients are not "employed by the University." Rather, "they receive benefits based upon their past demonstrated ability." Thus, the court reasoned, it was apparent that the university, the NCAA, the IRS, and Rensing did not consider the scholarship to be income. Rensing therefore could not be an employee within the meaning of the act.

Additionally, the court voiced approval of dissenting Judge Young's conclusion that Rensing was not "in the service of" the university, pointing out that most other courts would probably agree: "Courts in other jurisdictions have generally found that such individuals as student athletes, student leaders in student government associations and student resident-hall assistants are not 'employees' for purposes of workmen's compensation laws unless they are also employed in a university job in addition to receiving scholarship benefits."

According to the Indiana Supreme Court, the facts showed that Rensing did not receive "pay" for playing football within the meaning of the Workmen's Compensation Act. Thus, "an essential element of the employer-employee relationship was missing in addition to the lack of intent." Moreover,

. . . under the applicable rules of the NCAA, Rensing's benefits could not be reduced or withdrawn because of his athletic ability or his contribution to the team's success. Thus, the ordinary employer's right to discharge on the basis of performance was also missing. While there was an agreement between Rensing and the Trustees which established certain obligations for both parties, the agreement was not a contract of employment. Since at least three important factors indicative of an employee-employer relationship are absent in this case, we find it is not necessary to consider other factors which may or may not be present.

. . . the evidence here shows that Rensing enrolled at Indiana State University as a full-time student seeking advanced educational opportunities. He was not considered to be a professional athlete who was being paid for his athletic ability. In fact, the benefits Rensing received were subject to strict regulations by the NCAA which were designed to protect his amateur status. Rensing held no other job with the University and therefore cannot be considered an "employee" of the University within the meaning of the Workmen's Compensation Act.

It is our conclusion of law, under the facts here, including all rules and regulations of the University and the NCAA governing student athletes, that the appellant shall be considered only as a student athlete and not as an employee within the meaning of the Workmen's Compensation Act. Accordingly, we find that there is substantial evidence to support the finding of the Industrial Board that there was no employee-employer relationship between Rensing and the Trustees, and their finding must be upheld.

The Indiana Supreme Court opinion in Rensing is deficient in a number of respects. At the outset, the court acknowledges the propriety of a liberal construction of the worker's compensation statute and proceeds to apply a construction which is anything but liberal. But even if a liberal construction was not called for, the court's opinion invites criticism. The court's analysis of the intent of the parties raises a number of problems. The probable reality of the situation is that neither the athlete nor the institution granting the scholarship gave the employee-employer question much thought. The holding, however, turns on the lack of a "mutual belief" concerning a matter that the parties, in all likelihood, did not consciously consider at all. In such a case, a better approach would be to assess the nature of the relationship created by the contract, which is exactly what the Court of Appeals did when it concluded that Rensing really was an employee. After all, the court concluded, Rensing and the university "bargained for an exchange in the manner of employer and employee." The Supreme Court's conclusion that the requisite intent was lacking gives short shrift to the contractual relationship created by the scholarship, which is the best evidence of the intent of the parties.

At the same time, the court gives great weight to the fact that the NCAA constitution and bylaws were incorporated by reference into Rensing's contract. This agreement to incorporate, according to the court, is a clear manifestation of Rensing's intent not to be regarded as an employee for worker's compensation purposes. This is an unconvincing judicial stretch of the imagination. It is difficult to see how the intent of the parties, in incorporating these documents, was to reflect agreement that Rensing was not to be treated as an employee for worker's compensation purposes. Similarly, just because the IRS does not consider a scholarship as taxable income does not necessarily mean that the recipient is not an employee for worker's compensation purposes.

To say that Rensing was not "in the service of" the university and did not receive "pay" flies in the face of the plain meanings of those words. To say that Rensing could not be discharged on the basis of performance is simply a misstatement of fact which contradicts common experience in the amateur sports setting.

ADDITIONAL NOTES

1. *The jockey cases. Gross v. Pellicane* refers to a series of other cases dealing with the issue of whether free-lance jockeys are employees for worker's compensation purposes. *Gross* reflects the majority view that free-lance jockeys are employees. A couple of alternative views, however, should be noted.

In a case cited in *Gross, Moore v. Clarke*, 171 Md. 39, 187 A. 887 (1936), the Maryland court held that a free-lance jockey is a "casual" employee, not sufficiently connected with any employer to justify the conclusion that worker's compensation coverage is warranted. And in an Illinois case subsequent to *Gross, Clark v. Industrial Commission*, 54 Ill. 2d 311, 297 N.E.2d 154 (1973), a free-lance jockey was viewed as being an independent contractor not covered by the worker's compensation scheme. On its facts, *Clark* is not distinguishable in a meaningful way from *Gross*.

2. It is not entirely clear that the court in *Gross*, however, is correct in concluding that the free-lance jockey was an employee of the trainer and not of the owner. Since it was undisputed that the obligation to pay the jockey was on the owners, a sound argument can be made that the owners were the real employers. There is a paucity of reported cases on this issue, which, for the time being, is perhaps best viewed as unsettled.

3. Weistart and Lowell state "the jockey . . . cases should also provide a sufficient basis of authority to enable the courts to make similar determinations with regard to other types of non-team sport professional athletes" at 1013. In this regard, however, recall the admonition in *Gross*: "The status . . . is to be resolved upon the totality of the facts surrounding the relationship, with due regard for the attendant circumstances, the object in view, and the course of practice in its execution."

4. *Nemeth* and *Dennison* seem indistinguishable. Both athletes re-

ceived university benefits (pay) in exchange for participation in football. This writer contends that scholarship athletes are in fact "paid" to participate in sports.

5. *Scholarship athletes as university employees.* The litmus test of whether a college athlete should be considered an employee for worker's compensation purposes is the existence of a quid pro quo arrangement. When competent evidence shows that the student's performance of athletic services is given as consideration for financial aid, the courts should recognize the student's status as a student-employee. *Nemeth* and *Van Horn* have recognized the reality of this contractual relationship.

An objective appraisal of the relevant cases reveals the better-reasoned approach: the ordinary athletic scholarship does indeed create an employer-employee relationship. For a variety of unarticulated reasons—foremost among them the fear of uncharted waters—it is not surprising that the courts in the past have refused, and will in the future refuse, to hold that the amateur athletes are really employees. It is an uncomfortable and unsettling realization that our scholarship athletes are really employees, but it is a conclusion that an honest appraisal compels. And it is a conclusion from which a number of beneficial consequences will undoubtedly flow, contributing to the reform of a system much in need of constructive change:

a. One immediate consequence of course is that athletes in Rensing's position will be compensated for athletic injuries. As things stand now, athletes such as Rensing on our college campuses can only recover for injuries suffered by either pursuing tort remedies or counting on the largesse of the university community. The tort remedy will often be unavailable because of the absence of negligence. The availability of voluntary assistance is haphazard. The worker's compensation model is the obvious mechanism for granting relief. Some kind of insurance fund for injured athletes must be provided.

b. If scholarship athletes really are university employees, they are not "amateurs" as that term is commonly defined. To a certain extent this means that big-time college sports will be openly professionalized. In the eyes of many who have studied the current system, this would be a healthy development. The American Council on Education, for example, recently issued an internal report following a study of the American amateur sports system. The Council is a research group representing some 1,400 colleges and universities. The Council, after noting the "corruption" that is rampant in major college football and basketball programs, suggested that a solution is for the major college football and basketball powers to shed the facade of amateurism, pay athletes over the table, and not even require them to be students. The report stated that the situation was beyond the control of the National Collegiate Athletic Association. College presidents, according to the report, faced three options: (1) *A return to amateurism* (This option, however, was regarded as "not really viable" because of economic pressures and demands from alumni and other supporters for winning teams.); (2) *Continuing the present situation* (The Council noted that continuing the status quo meant drifting toward professionalism and an increased credibility gap between the pretenses of the student athlete model and the realities of money, corruption, and professionalism.); or (3) *An open move to professionalism* (This entails a situation in which blue-chip athletes would be paid a market wage rather than an artificially constrained amount with all the attendant pressures for under-the-table payments.).

The Council favored the third option, which in turn would create an environment in which true amateurism could be reborn. Schools that do not desire professional teams could opt for a genuine amateur model and build organizations capable of being administered in a principled manner.

Courts contribute to the maintenance of an admittedly corrupt system by abdicating their responsibility to call things as they really must see them (as the Indiana Supreme Court did in *Rensing*). Courts willing to honestly appraise the present relationships in American "amateur" sports must conclude that our big-time college scholarship athletes are really employees. This honest appraisal might, in turn, lead to healthy reform.

6. Finally, note that suits by under-educated college athletes alleging what can loosely be described as "educator's malpractice" deserve sympathetic hearings. Success in such cases might also contribute to reform of the current system.

BIBLIOGRAPHY

Ashman, Allan, "Hut One, hut two, no comp for you: College Football Injury Doesn't Qualify for Worker's Compensation, *Rensing v. Indiana State University Board of Trustees*, 444 N.E.2d 1170 (Ind. 1983)," 69 AMERICAN BAR ASSOCIATION JOURNAL 828 (June 1983).

Bouniconti, Nicholas A., "Are Athletes Covered by Worker's Compensation?" 13 THE BRIEF 4 (November 1983).

Cross, Harry M., "The College Athlete and the Institution," 38 LAW AND CONTEMPORARY PROBLEMS 151, 163–66 (1973).

Holzberg, Bryan, "Worker's Compensation for Students," 4 NATIONAL LAW JOURNAL 6 (July 5, 1982).

Steinbach, Sheldon Elliot, "Workmen's Compensation and the Scholarship Athlete," 19 CLEVELAND STATE LAW REVIEW 521 (1970).

"Workmen's Compensation Awards for Recreational Injuries," 23 UNIVERSITY OF CHICAGO LAW REVIEW 328 (1956).

"Workmen's Compensation—Recreational Injuries," 24 TENNESSEE LAW RE-
VIEW 870 (1957).
Yasser, Ray, "Are Scholarship Athletes at Big-Time Programs Really University
Employees?-You Bet They Are!" 9 BLACK LAW JOURNAL 65 (1984).

7

Intentional Interference with Contractual Relations

Extraordinarily talented people are often in demand. This is particularly true when the talent is marketable. When this is the case, it is not unusual to see employers vying for the services of a peculiarly gifted person. This in turn gives rise to the classic-fact pattern out of which arises the intentional interference with contractual relations tort. The landmark case of *Lumley v. Gye*, 118 Eng. Rep. 749 (1853) is illustrative of the classic-fact pattern. In that case, opera star Johanna Wagner had entered into an exclusive contract to perform for the Queen's Theatre. The Queen's Theatre alleged that the defendant, a rival employer, had attempted to induce Johanna Wagner to refuse to perform for the Queen's Theatre. In a case that broke new ground, the court recognized intentional interference with contractual relations as a viable cause of action. The tort today retains special vitality in the sports setting as rival employers typically vie for the special services of especially gifted athletes and coaches.

The tort's modern profile requires the plaintiff to show that the defendant intentionally interfered with an existing contractual relationship of the plaintiff. The defendant must do something that either prevents performance of the contract or makes performance substantially less likely. The defendant must have actual knowledge of the contract and must act with the intention of interfering with the contract. The defendant can justify the interference by showing that, on balance, his right to compete with the plaintiff for the personal services of others outweighs the plaintiff's interest in entirely stable contractual relations. Thus, the defendant might be justified in seeking to open negotiations with someone who is already employed. The cases which follow explore the parameters of the tort in greater detail.

Also, a separate cause of action against the employee often accompanies the claim of intentional interference with contractual relations. Typically, the plaintiff in the contractual relations claim will also seek to enjoin the employee from performing for someone else. This "negative injunction" is a standard remedial tool in the entertainment and sports industries. To illustrate, note that *Lumley v. Gye* had a companion, *Lumley v. Wagner* 42 Eng. Rep. 687 (1852). In that case, the Queen's Theatre sought injunctive relief against Johanna Wagner to force her to perform her contract and to prevent her from performing elsewhere. The court held that while Johanna could not be compelled to perform for the Queen's Theatre, she could be prevented from performing elsewhere. This is generally true today in the sports industry.

THE LANDMARK CASES

World Football League v. Dallas Cowboys Football Club, Inc.
513 S.W.2d 102 (Tex. Civ. App. 1974)

[At the time of the lawsuit, the World Football League (WFL) was a newly organized professional football league attempting to compete with the well-established National Football League (NFL). The Dallas Cowboys, a franchised NFL team, sought injunctive relief against WFL recruiting practices which it characterized as "raiding." In particular, the Cowboys complained about letters and return postcards that were sent by the WFL to players under contract with the Cowboys, urging the players to consider signing with a WFL team. In pertinent part, the letter read as follows:

Dear Player:

The World Football League will begin play in 1974 with franchises in twelve areas, including New York, Chicago, Detroit, Toronto, New England, Southern California, Hawaii and Florida. The remaining franchises will be awarded from some twenty applications for membership under consideration.

It is the intention of the World Football League to be "Major League" in every way, particularly in signing the top professional players available. We feel strongly that every player should honor his present contractual obligation. However, we would very much like to talk with you about the possibility of joining our League at the expiration of your present contract.

In order for us to know your status and to contact you, please fill out and return the enclosed post card as soon as possible.

· · · · · · · ·

The postcards asked for information about the player, including name, address, and number of years remaining on contract and asked the player to indicate if he was interested in hearing an offer from the WFL.

Three Cowboys (Calvin Hill, Craig Morton, and Mike Montgomery) signed WFL contracts to perform for WFL teams following the completion of their contractual obligations to the Cowboys. The Cowboys argued that the WFL was guilty of tortious interference with contractual relations and were granted injunctive relief at the trial court level. The Court of Civil Appeals here dissolved the temporary injunction.]

· · · · · · · ·

The Club argues that WFL is guilty of "pirating" its players and that unless enjoined it will continue to do so, but the only evidence of any contact whatever between WFL and the Club's players is the above quoted letter and the post card enclosed therewith. These writings do not suggest an unlawful "raiding scheme." The letter plainly states that the player should honor his existing contractual obligations and inquires only about the possibility of the player's interest in joining one of the WFL teams after the expiration of his present contract. There was no evidence of legal malice or deceitful means used by WFL or any motive or effort on its part to interfere with the contractual relations between the Club and its players.

The Club also contends that WFL arranged for, and induced three players to participate in, press conferences and various publicity activities surrounding the signing of contracts with WFL teams by Hill, Morton and Montgomery, thus causing a breach of the contracts between said players and the Club. In each of those contracts the player agrees "that during the term of this contract he will play football and engage in activities related to football only for the Club." . . .

The Club's principal contention is that the signing of the Cowboy players by WFL teams for services to be rendered after expiration of their present contracts is an unlawful interference with the Club's present contractual relations with its players, as defined by the above provision of its contracts, because the players so signing will not use their best efforts for the team under their current contracts, the morale of the entire team will suffer, the enthusiasm of the fans will wane, and the new employers will reap the benefits of any favorable publicity for outstanding performance of the players so signing. The Club argues further that publicity resulting from the signing of such contracts for future services is a breach of the present obligations which the players owe to the Club.

These facts, even if true, do not present grounds for equitable relief. We must consider the freedom of contract of the individual players as well as the rights of the Club under its present contracts. Bargaining for future services is a matter of economics. The Club can assure itself of the continued services and loyalty of its players by offering them long-term contracts and other financial inducements. If it chooses not to do so for economic reasons, it has no legal ground to complain if the players look elsewhere for their future careers and enter into contracts for services to be performed when their present contracts with the Club expire. Signing such contract is neither a breach of the contract by the players nor a tortious interference by the future employers, and the threat to enter into such contracts affords no ground for equitable relief. Neither does the publicity necessarily attendant upon the signing of contracts with well-known players constitute a tort. An injunction restraining the signing of such contracts because of the attendant publicity would be an unreasonable restraint on the freedom of contract of the players and their prospective employers.

We should not be understood, however, as holding that other promotional and publicity activities for the benefit of future employers would not be subject to restraint as "activities relating to football," which the players are bound by their present contracts to reserve for the Club. No such limited equitable relief was sought either in the trial court or in this court. The Club has cast its entire case for injunctive relief on its contention that the signing of contracts for future services would in itself be a tortious interference with the players' performance of their obligations under their present contracts with the Club. Since the injunction cannot be sustained on that ground, it must be dissolved.

· · · · · · · ·

The temporary injunction is dissolved.

New England Patriots Football Club, Inc. v. University of Colorado
592 F.2d 1196 (1st Cir. 1979)

[In 1973 Chuck Fairbanks contracted with the New England Patriots, a professional football club in the National Football League, to act as its general manager and head coach. In so doing, Fairbanks breached his then existing contract with the University of Oklahoma. In 1977, Fairbanks' contract with the Patriots was extended through 1983. The contract contained a provision that Fairbanks would not provide services connected with football to any entity other than the Patriots. It also contained a provision that Fairbanks would not render services to another not connected with football except with the permission of the Patriots. In November of 1978, Fairbanks was approached by agents of the University of Colorado to become its head football coach. At first, the negotiations were secret. When Fairbanks agreed to terms with the

University of Colorado, he informed Sullivan, the owner of the Patriots, of his intention to leave the Patriots at the close of the 1978 season. Sullivan suspended Fairbanks and sought injunctive relief against
the University of Colorado. The district court entered a preliminary injunction enjoining the University of Colorado from causing the university to employ Fairbanks as the university's coach. The university appealed, and Fairbanks was given permission to file an amicus brief. The
First Circuit here affirmed the district court.]

Although this is not our first experience with the athletic milieu's response to legal embroilment engendered by contract jumping, [foot-
note omitted] we set out the factual contentions in some detail in order
to get in the mood. For this opportunity we are primarily indebted to
the Fairbanks amicus brief. [Footnote omitted.]

The extension of the contract to January 26, 1983 was agreed to on
June 6, 1977. The briefs are silent as to this date, an understandable
reticence in view of the fact that by that time Fairbanks had, apparently, already decided he might not keep his word.

"For a number of years, Fairbanks was extremely unhappy with remaining in
professional football [and] . . . with his present location . . . Fairbanks believed the health of his family, and a reassessment of career objectives, *mandated a change*. Accordingly, for a number of years, he had been investigating
business opportunities outside football, as well as coaching at the college level,
. . . " (Amicus br. 8) (Emphasis suppl.) . . .

. . . Because in 1973 the Patriots allegedly had lured Fairbanks from
the University of Oklahoma, inducing him to break his contract there,
defendants conclude that the Patriots are barred from relief by the doctrine of unclean hands. We disagree. Both parties may have done the
University of Oklahoma dirt, but that does not mean unclean hands
with respect to "the controversy in issue."

Equally, we are not taken by Fairbanks' claim that because, when he
told Sullivan that he was leaving at the end of the season and Sullivan
responded that he was "suspended," it was Sullivan who broke the
contract.

"The simple fact is that Fairbanks was fired." (Amicus br. 11).

Whatever may be thought the meaning in the trade of suspension,
as distinguished from its commonly understood meaning, it is a novel
concept that a contract-breaker had the option to require the other party
to accept his choice of dates. At least until Fairbanks withdrew his unlawful announcement, the Patriots had a right not to accept the services of an unfaithful servant, or, as Sullivan put it to him at the time,
one who had "his body in Foxboro and his heart in Colorado." [Foot-
note omitted.]

· · · · · · · ·

At the hearing Fairbanks testified that although the contract read "services directly connected with football . . . [or for] another entity not connected with football," this meant, simply, activities competitively connected with the Patriots. Apparently he has no more regard for the parole evidence rule forbidding the contradiction of unambiguous language than for other rules foisted upon him by legalisms. Parenthetically, having in mind, as sometimes helpless dial-spinners, that professional and prominent college football teams compete for TV viewers, and hence, presumably, for the advertising dollar, we may wonder whether we have to accept at face value the protestation of no competitive activity here. In any event, there is ample authority contradicting both aspects of defendants' legal position. Indeed, some courts have gone even further, and have enjoined the defaulting athlete himself from noncompetitive sport. *E.G., Munchak v. Cunningham*, 4th Cir., 1972, 457 F.2d 721 (ABA player enjoined from play with NBA, prior to merger); *Houston Oilers, Inc. v. Neely*, ante (AFL player enjoined from NFL play, prior to merger); *Nassau Sports v. Peters*, E.D.N.Y., 1972, 352 F.Supp. 870 (NHL player enjoined from play in fledgling WHA); *Winnipeg Rugby Football Club v. Freeman*, N.D. Ohio, 1955, 140 F.Supp. 365 (player under contract to Canadian team and NFL team enjoined); *see also Boston Professional Hockey Ass'n v. Cheevers*, ante (chance of irreparable harm shown by players under contract with NHL team jumping to WHA); *American League Baseball Club v. Pasquel*, Sup. Ct., 1946, 187 Misc. 230, 63 N.Y.S.2d 537 (Mexican League enjoined from inducing American League players from repudiating contracts). We would not distinguish between an athlete and a coach. To enjoin tortious interference by a third party, whether or not competitive, would seem a lesser step. *See Winnipeg Rugby Football Club v. Freeman*, ante; *Pino v. Trans-Atlantic Marine, Inc.*, 1970, 358 Mass. 498, 265 N.E.2d 583; *Moore Drop Forging Co. v. McCarthy*, 1923, 243 Mass. 554, 137 N.E. 919; *American League Baseball Club v. Pasquel*, ante.

· · · · · · · ·

We comment briefly on the self-serving statement in Fairbanks' amicus brief that he is "through with professional football." There is no such finding in the record, and even though that may now be the conventional wisdom, neither the Patriots nor the court are bound to accept it. At this stage Fairbanks could be expected to say no less. Defendants' constant stress that the injunction is unproductive, and nothing but "punishment" in light of the fact that a position with the University "is the only game in town," is a total non-sequitur that cuts the other way. If there may, in part, be a punitive effect, we could not avoid wondering how great a miscarriage that would be with respect to one who, on his own testimony, promised a longer term than he intended to keep, not only to afford himself sanctuary while he looked around, but, again on his own testimony, putting himself in line for higher pay meanwhile, and whose seeming only defense to his announced total breach is a claim that the Patriots grabbed the gun.

· · · · · · · ·

A CASE STUDY—*CINCINNATI BENGALS, INC. v. BERGEY* 453 F. Supp. 129 (S.D. Ohio, 1974) *aff'd*, Civil No. 74–1570 (6th Cir. Aug. 27, 1974)

The case is in many ways similar to *World Football League v. Dallas Cowboys Football Club*. But the attack on the World Football League (WFL) recruiting practices by the National Football League (NFL) Cincinnati Bengals (Bengals) franchise has a broader base, and issues not addressed in the *Cowboys* case are confronted directly here.

The Bengals' offense. On the field, the Bengals are noted for their creatively successful offense. This philosophy carries over to their litigation. The gist of the Bengals' claim is that the WFL, and its member teams, are tortiously invading the Bengals' ranks by signing players under existing Bengal contracts to contracts for future services. The Bengals seek injunctive relief, contending that the WFL is irreparably harming the Bengals by intentionally interfering with existing contractual relations. One key argument made by the Bengals is that a player who signs a contract for future services with the WFL is likely to "dog it" with the Bengals. Another key argument is that these signings adversely affect the performance of the rest of the team.

More particularly, the Bengals objected to the WFL's signing of two players, Steve Chomyszak and Bill Bergey. On April 9, 1974, Chomyszak signed a contract to play with the WFL Philadelphia Bell. The contract provided that Chomyszak would begin playing for the Bell at the conclusion of his contract with the Bengals following the 1974 season unless the Bengals released him in which case the WFL contract would "accelerate." Since the Bell had agreed to pay Chomyszak more than the Bengals, the Bengals argued that Chomyszak had an incentive to be "cut" by the Bengals in order to start playing for the Bell.

Bergey was under contract with the Bengals through May 1976 at a salary of $38,750 per year. On April 17, 1974, Bergey signed with the WFL Virginia Ambassadors. The contract provided that Bergey would begin playing with the Ambassadors in May 1976, at a salary of $125,000 per year. Like Chomyszak's contract, Bergey's had an "acceleration" clause which provided: "However, should Bergey be released from his contract with The Cincinnati Bengals, Inc. so as to be available for the entire 1974 and 1975 football season, then, in such event, the term of this contract shall cover the 1974, 1975 and 1976 football seasons or the 1975, 1976 and 1977 football seasons, as the case may be." Additionally, Bergey's contract paid him a $150,000 bonus in consideration of signing. And finally, it was a "no-cut" contract, payable even in the event that Bergey was cut from the team for lack of skill. Once again, the Bengals argued that this contract substantially interfered with their contract with Bergey because of the strong incentive it provided Bergey to be released by the Bengals.

In order to show the full effects of these signings, the Bengals introduced evidence concerning the nature of professional football. Bengals' coach Paul Brown testified that the success of a football team "comes down to nothing, really, but people" and that "if they're ever a bad character or boozer or chaser or what not, we're that much farther away from winning what we're trying to win." Coach Mike McCormick, of the Philadelphia Eagles, testified that the "individual sometimes has to suppress himself for the good of the team." He further testified: "I believe it's a game where, as the immediate supervisor, the head coach has to have control. I believe if a man is under contract to someone else, then that leverage and control has been taken away from the head coach."

McCormick testified that he believed that Bergey would be a divisive force on the Bengals. Four assistant coaches for the Bengals and one player elaborated on the theme. Football was a unique sport that required emotional commitments from every player to play with desire as a member of a cohesive unit. Contractual commitments to WFL teams tended to destroy this commitment. The trial judge concluded: "From all this the Court can and does find that football is probably unique in that, to a greater degree than other professional sports, it is a team sport. Also it takes time and money to develop the players and 'units' so that they will be cohesive. In short, football is a scientific, sophisticated sport, and a delicate sort of mechanism."

In summary, the Bengals argued that these signings had a detrimental effect not only on Bergey's and Chomyszak's performances, but on the other members of the team as well.

The WFL defense. In an effort to disprove the requisite intent to interfere with contractual relations, the WFL offered testimony that the signing of name players to future contracts was essential to the WFL's success. The WFL was not trying to interfere with existing contractual relations; it was attempting to gain public acceptance as a bona fide professional football league. The court specifically acknowledged that "starting a new league is a risky business" and found that "the WFL's motive for signing established NFL players is not to cause any harm to the NFL teams in general or the Cincinnati Bengals in particular, but to further the competitive interests of the WFL."

The WFL also introduced evidence to offset the Bengals' claim that the signing had a detrimental effect on team performance. Several players testified specifically that Bergey's performance was not noticeably altered by his signing. The gist of the WFL testimony in this regard was that the signings had no appreciable detrimental effect on team performance. Assistant Coach Chuck Studley admitted that he perceived no animosity among the Bengals as a result of the lawsuit and that neither team morale nor team performance had suffered.

Discussion

The Intent Requirement

The court found that "the WFL's motive for signing established NFL players is not to cause any harm to the NFL teams in general or the Cincinnati Bengals in particular, but to further the competitive interests of the WFL." The court also found that the evidence was insufficient to justify the conclusion that "the WFL has singled out the Cincinnati Bengals as a target of destruction the accomplishment of which is through improper interference with the contracts between the Bengals and its players, nor that the WFL seeks to destroy the National Football League by its actions." Since the WFL was not shown to have used "deceitful means," there was no evidence of "legal malice" sufficient to make out a claim of intentional interference with contractual relations.

It must be pointed out that the *Bergey* court's conclusion in this regard is not mandated by modern authority. The Bergey court, in fact, represents a minority view in its insistence that some kind of "malice" or "deceit" be shown. Although the earlier cases appeared to require ill will, the modern trend, as Weistart and Lowell point out, "is toward defining the malice element to require only that the third party acted in knowing disregard of the plaintiff's rights under the existing contract, without further qualification as to the acceptability of . . . motive" at 405. This is not saying that the *Bergey* court was erroneous in concluding that the requisite intention had not been shown, but only suggesting that a good many courts might well have gone the other way. It is also interesting to note that the *Bergey* court ignored the "acceleration" clauses in both Bergey's and Chomyszak's contracts. These clauses seem to be particularly relevant on the issue of WFL intent. Surely someone offering such a clause must know of its likely effect on performance.

The Interference with Contractual Relations

The court correctly noted that there is uniform agreement that a rival employer may contract for services to commence at the expiration of the existing contract. Recognizing that player loyalty might be marginally affected, any other conclusion would unduly restrict a player's ability to market his services. The gist of the tort is that the rival employer must interfere in a substantial way with existing contractual relations. Contracts for future services are thought not to substantially interfere with existing contracts.

Once again, the acceleration clauses are particularly relevant. The court rejected the plaintiff's argument that the acceleration clause of Bergey's WFL contract would induce Bergey to seek his release prior to the expiration of his NFL contract, accepting "as true Bergey's testimony that he has no intention of seeking an early release." The court concluded that "there is *no* incentive to Bergey to compromise with his pride in his playing ability which impels him to be the aggressive player that he is" (emphasis mine). Because Bergey stood to receive an immediate annual raise of over $86,000 if the Bengals released him, the court's wholehearted acceptance of Bergey's testimony is disingenuous. The court was apparently blinded by the glare of Bergey's stardom. Once again, a good argument can be made that such acceleration clauses in fact tortiously interfere with existing contractual relations. Indeed, Chomyszak admitted that he wanted to free himself of his obligation to the Bengals. The court found this admission unconvincing.

The court was probably correct in concluding that the signings would not have a significantly divisive effect on the team. In this regard, the court found it "unlikely" that Bergey's signing would have "a detrimental effect on the performance of player morale of the Bengals as a whole." The court, however, did note, in dicta, that a cause of action could be stated if "a sizeable group of starting players were under contract to another team." Thus, the court left the litigation door open in situations in which the new employer contracts with several players on the same team.

Conclusion

The tort of intentional interference with contractual relations requires an accommodation of competing interests. On the one hand is the value of stability in existing contractual relations. On the other hand is the rival employer's right to compete for services. The real issue in many of these cases is whether the rival employer's competitive tactics are acceptable or not. The *Bergey* court implicitly approved the acceleration clauses. Many others would, I think, find such clauses unacceptable.

ADDITIONAL NOTES

1. Before a "negative injunction" will issue preventing a player from performing elsewhere, the court must be convinced that the person

against whom relief is sought is a person of exceptional and unique knowledge, skill, and ability. Whether a professional athlete is, automatically, such a person is subject to controversy. *Central New York Basketball, Inc. v. Barnett*, 19 Ohio App. 2d 130, 181 N.E.2d 506 (1961) suggests that he is. *Matuszak v. Houston Oilers, Inc.*, 515 S.W.2d 725 (Tex. Civ. App. 1974) says it depends on the facts of the case.

Richard Barnett was the number one draft pick of the Syracuse Nationals in 1959. (New York Knick fans may recall that Barnett later earned the nickname "Fall Back Baby" because that was the phrase he uttered right after launching his extremely idiosynchratic jump shot. Barnett would say "fall back baby" to prevent other players from wasting their energy by vying for a rebound that was, in Barnett's opinion, not to come.) Barnett signed and played with the Nationals and then tried to jump to the Cleveland franchise in the newly organized American Basketball League. The Nats were able to prevent the jump. On the issue of the uniqueness of Barnett's skills, the trial court admitted testimony from a number of basketball experts. The general manager of the Syracuse team thought Barnett was "one of the greatest." The Cleveland coach testified that Barnett was "pretty good." Barnett himself did not think his talents were unique and testified that he was not, in his opinion, as good as Oscar Robertson. After reviewing the testimony, the court, perhaps recognizing the futility of it all, concluded that, on the issue of uniqueness, "players in the major leagues have unusual talents and skills or they would not be so employed."

John Matuszak was the National Football League's number one draft pick in 1973 and signed to play with the Houston Oilers. He subsequently tried to jump to the Texans of the newly organized World Football League. The Oilers were able to get temporary injunctive relief which prevented Matuszak from playing with the Texans. An appeal was taken by the Texans. On appeal, the Texas Court of Civil Appeals had occasion to discuss "uniqueness." The court thought that "uniqueness" or "non-uniqueness" was properly viewed as a fact question to be decided on a player-by-player basis.

2. Another prerequisite to injunctive relief is that the party seeking it possess "clean hands." This in turn has on occasion meant that one seeking injunctive relief must not have engaged in tortious conduct. While it is fairly well established that one's hands are not sullied by negotiating with a player under contract for services to be performed at the expiration of the existing contract, a number of questions remain concerning just what type of conduct sufficiently soils the hands. A quick review of the leading cases follows.

a. In *Munchak Corp. v. Cunningham*, 331 F. Supp. 872 (M.D. N.C. 1971), rev'd, 457 F.2d 721 (4th Cir. 1972), Billy Cunningham was under contract to play for the Philadelphia 76ers during the 1969–1970 season. This contract contained an option clause which gave the 76ers the right to renew the contract for another year—a practice common in the sports industry. Under the terms of the 1969–1970 contract, Cunningham was paid $55,000. The option year salary could not be less than 75 percent of $55,000.

While Cunningham was under contract with the 76ers, the Carolina Cougars (a team in the competing league, the American Basketball Association) entered into negotiations with Cunningham. The negotiation ripened into a three-year contract to commence at the expiration of Cunningham's option year contract. Under the terms of the Cougar contract, Cunningham received over $100,000 per year. He also received a $125,000 signing bonus, $45,000 which was paid immediately. The remaining $80,000 was subject to a rather unusual agreement between the Cougars and Cunningham. Under the terms of the agreement, if Cunningham played for the 76ers during his option year, the Cougars would pay only as much of the $80,000 as was necessary to bring Cunningham's salary up to $100,000. If Cunningham chose to sit out his option year, then he would receive the full $80,000.

In the complicated litigation that ensued, Cunningham tried to get out of the Cougar contract. One of his claims was that the Cougars lacked clean hands and were therefore not entitled to injunctive relief. The court found nothing objectionable about the agreement concerning the payment of the signing bonus. It noted that the Cougars did not interfere with the contractual rights of the 76ers since the contract actually provided an incentive to Cunningham to play for the 76ers during his option year. The court reasoned that the provision calling for the $80,000 payment if Cunningham sat out the option year was not a tortious interference with the 76ers' rights since Cunningham had every right to sit out his option year if he so desired. Moreover, the court pointed out, sitting out would cost him $20,000 under the agreement.

It should be noted that the court really misperceived the arrangement Cunningham had with the Cougars. The agreement really did encourage Cunningham not to play the option year, not to risk getting hurt, and to just sit back, collect $80,000, and wait for the lucrative contract with the Cougars to ripen. The court, I think, was incorrect in concluding that the Cougars did not tortiously interfere with the contractual rights of the 76ers.

b. Compare *Washington Capitols Basketball Club, Inc. v. Barry*, 304 F. Supp. 1193 (N.D. Cal. 1969), *aff'd*, 419 F.2d 472 (9th Cir. 1969), with *Minnesota Muskies, Inc. v. Hudson*, 294 F. Supp. 979 (M.D.N.C. 1969). Rick Barry began his professional basketball career in San Francisco playing for the NBA Warriors. At the termination of that contract, Barry signed with the ABA Oakland Oaks for three years. After the first year of the contract, the Oaks were sold, and the franchise was moved to

Washington, D.C., and renamed the Capitols. Upon receiving news of the franchise shift, Barry signed a contract with the NBA Warriors for a term overlapping with his ABA contract. The Capitols in turn brought suit to prevent Barry from playing for the Warriors and were successful in securing injunctive relief against Barry. Barry's allegation that the Oaks should not receive equitable relief because of "unclean hands" (for having lured Barry away from the Warriors) was unavailing. The court stated the now well-established principle that there is nothing "unclean" or tortious about negotiating for services to commence after the termination of a preexisting contract.

Under remarkably similar facts, the court in *Hudson* denied injunctive relief to the Minnesota Muskies on the ground that they lacked clean hands because they induced Hudson to breach his existing contract by agreeing to pay Hudson to sit out. The court found "unwarranted interference" and an "inducement to repudiate" where the *Barry* court did not.

c. Is it an interference with existing contractual relations for the soon-to-be employer to publicize the fact that a player has agreed to "jump"? The issue was touched upon briefly in both *Dallas Cowboys* and *Bergey*. Both courts thought that the publicity which necessarily flowed from the signing was unavoidable and obviously not tortious. But a number of questions remain. While the player would apparently be able to attend a press conference to announce his intention to play for the new club at some later date, may the new club enlist the player to promote ticket sales while the player is still under contract to his old club? May the new club prevail upon the player to attend promotional events? Or would this be a tortious interference with the existing contractual relations of the old club?

3. Thus far, the question of intentional interference has come up in the classic *Lumley v. Gye* context. That is to say, the basic ingredient is a rival, competing employer wooing away employees under contract. Is the context the same when it involves a rival employer who attempts to convince the employee to play a wholly different game? By way of illustration, take the Danny Ainge case. Ainge is under contract to play baseball for the Toronto Blue Jays. Red Auerbach, general manager of the Celtics, tries to convince Ainge to play basketball instead. Is Red's conduct to be evaluated as though he was trying to get Ainge to play baseball for him? Or is Red's competitive privilege broader in this context?

4. Most of the professional leagues have bylaws which prohibit a club from "tampering" with players on other teams. The standard provision makes it improper for a club to "tamper, negotiate with, or make an offer to" a player under contract with another club (NFL Constitution and Bylaws, Art. 9.2 (1972)). The typical sanctions are losses of draft

choices and fines. With such rules, the leagues deter conduct which is legitimate under applicable tort principles. Note that the no-tampering rules, for example, would prohibit negotiating for future services, which is clearly not tortious.

BIBLIOGRAPHY

Alyulia, Kenneth, "Professional Sports Contracts and the Players Association," 5 MANITOBA LAW JOURNAL 359 (1973).

Brennan, James T., "Injunctions Against Professional Athletes Breaching Their Contracts," 34 BROOKLYN LAW REVIEW 61 (1967).

"Contract Matters and Disciplinary Procedures in Professional Sport," 39 SASKATCHEWAN LAW REVIEW 213 (1975).

"Contractual Rights and Duties of the Professional Athlete—Playing the Game in a Bidding War," 77 DICKINSON LAW REVIEW 352 (1972–73).

"Enforceability of Professional Sports Contracts—What's the Harm in It?" 35 SOUTHWESTERN LAW JOURNAL 803 (1981).

"Enforcement Problems of Personal Service Contracts in Professional Athletics," 6 TULSA LAW JOURNAL 40 (1969).

"Equity—Injunctions—Negative Covenant in Personal Employment Contracts—Boxing," 5 NEW YORK LAW FORUM 456 (1969).

Gilroy, Thomas P. & Madden, Patrick J., "Labor Relations in Professional Sports," 28 LABOR LAW JOURNAL 268 (1977).

Heiner, S. Phillip, "Post Merger Blues: Intra-League Contract Jumping," 18 WILLIAM & MARY LAW REVIEW 741 (1977).

"Injunction—Contract for Personal Services—Mutuality, *Philadelphia Ball Club v. Lajoie*, (S. Ct. Penn. 1902), *American Baseball & Athletic Exhibition Co. v. Harper*, (Cir. Ct. St. Louis 1902)," 54 CENTRAL LAW JOURNAL 449 (1902).

"Injunctions in Professional Athletes' Contracts—An Overused Remedy," 43 CONNECTICUT BAR JOURNAL 538 (1969).

"Offer Sheet: An Attempt to Circumvent NCAA Prohibition of Representational Contracts," 14 LOYOLA UNIVERSITY LAW REVIEW 187 (1980).

"Professional Athletic Contracts and the Injunctive Dilemma," 8 JOHN MARSHALL JOURNAL OF PRACTICE & PROCEDURE 437 (1975).

"Professional Football—Are Three One Year Agreements Signed at One Sitting Actually One Contract? Are Players 'Public Figures'? *Chuy v. Philadelphia Eagles Football Club*, 431 F. Supp. 254 (E.D. Pa. 1977)," 10 CONNECTICUT LAW REVIEW 350 (1978).

"Professional Sports: Involuntary Servitude and the Popular Will," 7 GONZAGA LAW REVIEW 63 (1971).

"Reserve Clauses in Athletic Contracts," 2 RUTGERS-CAMDEN LAW JOURNAL 302 (1970).

Sayre, F., "Inducing Breach of Contract," 36 HARVARD LAW REVIEW 663 (1923).

Tannenbaum, David, "Enforcement of Personal Service Contracts in the Entertainment Industry," 42 CALIFORNIA LAW REVIEW 18 (1954).

Table of Cases

Index

About the Author

RAYMOND L. YASSER is Professor of Law at the University of Tulsa College of Law. He has also served as an Assistant Attorney General for the State of North Carolina. He has published widely in the areas of torts, evidence, communications law, constitutional law, and sports law.